The SEN Handbook

for Trainee Teachers,
NQTs and TAs

Also available:

Mapping SEN
Routes through Identification to Intervention
Amanda Kirby
1-84312-327-4

Additional Educational Needs
Inclusive Approaches to Teaching
Sue Soan
1-84312-149-2

Professional Values and Practice
The Essential Guide for Higher Level Teaching Assistants
Anne Watkinson
1-84312-250-2

Professional Studies in the Primary School
Thinking Beyond the Standards
Eve English and Lynn Newton
1-84312-206-5

The SEN Handbook

for Trainee Teachers, NQTs and TAs

Wendy Spooner

 David Fulton Publishers

nasen
Helping Everyone Achieve

To the two Mikes without whom this book would never have been written.

David Fulton Publishers Ltd
The Chiswick Centre, 414 Chiswick High Road, London W4 5TF

www.fultonpublishers.co.uk

David Fulton Publishers is a division of Granada Learning, part of ITV plc.

British Library Cataloguing in Publication Data
A catalogue record for this book is available from the British Library.

ISBN: 1 84312 404 1

10 9 8 7 6 5 4 3 2 1

Typeset by RefineCatch Ltd, Bungay, Suffolk
Printed and bound in Great Britain

Contents

Foreword

There is nothing quite like the excitement of embarking upon a career in education, whether this be as a student teacher, teaching assistant or newly qualified teacher. The motivation to enter a profession committed to the education and development of young people, quite rightly, leads to an anticipation of enabling learners to make progress and the opportunity to share in their successes. Working with colleagues as part of a professional team assists in the gaining of confidence, and as more experience is gained the teacher or teaching assistant begins to recognise the difference which they make to the lives of young people.

However, conversations with colleagues in school, irrespective of their experience or qualifications, soon reveal that they are regularly challenged by pupils who appear to experience difficulties with learning. Many pupils recognise their own challenges and look to teachers and teaching assistants to help them in overcoming them. The commitment of professional colleagues to the acquisition of greater understanding of how pupils learn, the reasons why some find it difficult to respond, and the means of developing teaching which is both supportive and effective is a key factor in the success which has often been achieved when working with pupils with special educational needs. In this book, Wendy Spooner calls upon her own professional experience to provide practical advice to colleagues who are setting out on a journey to explore their own understanding of what it means to be an effective educator.

In recent years a focus upon approaches specifically designed to enable teachers and others to assist pupils to become better learners has led to an increased expectation of what might be achieved. In discussing these approaches and the principles upon which they are founded, Wendy Spooner provides clear insights into how we may move forward towards providing more inclusive classrooms. Texts such as this, clearly written and providing advice built upon a real understanding of classrooms and children, are needed at a time when colleagues in schools often feel overwhelmed by the day-to-day challenges they face. This book will not only encourage teachers and teaching assistants to examine their own practice but should also act as a catalyst for further investigation into the critical factors which enable children to learn.

Richard Rose
Director of the Centre for Special Needs Education and Research
University of Northampton
February 2006

Acknowledgements

This book would never have been written without the support and encouragement from NASEN colleagues, both past and present, and in particular, Barbara Pavey and Mike Gordon. I am also indebted to my David Fulton publisher Linda Evans.

School colleagues have been generous with their time, suggestions and examples of effective practice. I am particularly grateful to colleagues from three DfES Training Schools: Martin Sutton and Ann Mundie from Swanshurst Girls' School in Birmingham, Barbara Capstick from Bedgrove Infants School, Buckinghamshire and Nigel Palmer from Manor Park Primary School in Coventry.

I am very grateful to my son Jonathan for helping to check websites and contact details for the resources section. Last, but not least, I would like to thank my husband Mike, not only for his love, support and encouragement but also for using his librarian skills to compile the index.

Introduction

About this book

This book is about teaching and learning. It explores ways in which teaching and learning can be as effective as possible for *all* children and young people including those with a range of special needs. The three main aims of the book are:

1. To provide an introduction to special educational needs (SEN) for those training to be teachers, or for teaching assistants (TAs) or newly qualified teachers (NQTs) wanting to add to their knowledge and understanding about SEN.

2. To offer trainee teachers, newly qualified teachers, teaching assistants and those supporting them starting points and suggestions as to where to find further information, support and guidance.

3. To challenge and question readers' attitudes and thinking in relation to teaching and learning as a whole and to the needs of children and young people with special educational needs in particular.

What it covers

The first section of the book focuses on theory and issues. Chapter 1 considers the concept and legal definition of SEN and the historical context. It also introduces current legislation for England and the SEN Code of Practice (2001).

Chapter 2 takes a more detailed look at legislation in England and the SEN Code of Practice (2001) with the requirements of QTS Standard 2.6 for trainee teachers and HLTA Standard 2.8 particularly in mind.

Chapter 3 gives an overview of the Code of Practice's four areas of need together with the educational needs of the gifted and talented and children for whom English is an additional language (EAL).

Chapter 4 considers areas of common difficulty such as reading, writing and spelling, with a focus on the identification of needs, assessment and support across the age range.

Chapter 5 explores issues of inclusion and exclusion in the current social and legislative context.

Part 2 focuses on putting theory into practice. Chapter 6 considers general issues of teaching and learning as a context for the more specific exploration of effective teaching and learning for children with a range of educational needs.

Chapter 7 explores a range of teaching approaches including accelerated learning strategies and multi-sensory teaching.

Chapter 8 explores school-based training and issues relating to SEN which may arise when on school placements, together with some of the SEN issues NQTs are likely to meet. It also explores ways of keeping a balance so that learning and teaching is exciting and fulfilling for everyone in the classroom.

Although the needs of those training or working in schools and other educational settings in England have been highlighted, the underlying principles are equally applicable to other parts of the UK and beyond.

Appendix 1 provides further information about the professional standards for QTS and for HLTA in England.

How to use this book

Working through the book will provide you with an introduction to the concept of special educational needs within the broader educational context of teaching and learning. Taken as a whole, you will explore some of the issues and ideas from the perspective of a trainee teacher or a new teacher. The chapters build up to give you a broad overview of the main issues. You will find suggestions and pointers throughout to support you in working with pupils with a diversity of learning styles and educational needs across the Foundation, primary and secondary age ranges while you are on school placement or as you start out in your teaching career.

Dipping into a chapter will provide you with a starting point for further investigation into particular topics or issues. Some hints and tips are included, but this is not the main aim of the book. There are already a number of excellent and recently published books covering a range of needs which offer a wealth of practical guidance and ideas for the classroom. These are referred to in the text and details can be found in the Resources and further reading section.

For those training and working in England, the standards for Qualified Teacher Status (QTS) and for Higher Level Teaching Assistants (HLTAs), and the induction standards for Newly Qualified Teachers (NQTs) are to be found in the text margins next to relevant sections.

While in training there is an emphasis on identifying your own needs and areas for development. Similarly, there is an expectation that all those working in schools will take responsibility for their own professional development. Each chapter explores specific issues and includes a 'Reflection points' section with challenges and questions you might like to consider as part of your own professional development. For those in training, the questions may help you to think about your own attitudes and perspectives as well as giving you ideas for further investigation for assignments and your own professional needs. School- and university-based tutors may also find these to be useful stimuli for assignments, tasks and discussions.

However you use the book, I hope that it marks either the start or the continuation of your journey towards being an excellent and effective teacher or teaching assistant to all the pupils in your classes. The joy of teaching is in knowing that you have touched the lives of all the children with whom you come into contact as an education professional and that you have made a positive difference to their life chances.

PART 1

Theory and Issues

What are special educational needs?

In this chapter you will be introduced to the concept of special educational needs. A brief history of special educational needs to the present will provide the context for considering how attitudes and values have changed over the last 150 years.

QtT 1.1, 1.2, 1.3, 1.4

HLTA 1.1, 1.2, 1.3

At various points as you read, you will find questions or activities that are designed to help you to think about your own attitudes towards special educational needs and differences. Working through these will support you in meeting elements of Professional Values and Practice standards for both HLTA and QTS status.

Your personal starting point and attitude

I wonder what you feel is meant by a special educational need or the term 'special educational needs'. This will, of course, depend largely upon your past experiences and some readers will already be familiar with the legal definition. However, it is worth stopping for a moment to consider what the term means to you at this particular time.

What point are you starting from when thinking about this question? You may, for example, have a child or sibling with a disability, or you may perhaps have worked as a learning support assistant (LSA). In either case you will have direct experience, but perhaps within a limited field. For others, much of your knowledge and understanding may come from the media – television documentaries, films or magazine articles. Your attitude to children with special educational needs will also be coloured by your own experiences. If a family member is autistic or dyspraxic, for example, you may feel very differently about social or behavioural difficulties to someone who has had no experience of this at all.

Your attitude will have a major impact on how you respond to children in the classroom, as well as to their parents and other professionals, so it will be a recurrent theme in this book.

The personal audit in Figure 1.1 may help you to identify some of your feelings and attitudes. Put a cross on each line to mark what your current feeling or attitude is. You might like to come back to this at a later stage to see if anything has altered.

You are invited to put a cross on each line to mark how you currently feel.

1. My experience of being with people with special needs is . . .

   |___|___|___|___|___|___|___|___|___|___|

   non-existent or very limited   extensive

2. In general, my feelings about people with special needs are . . .

   |___|___|___|___|___|___|___|___|___|___|

   that I am unsure or   that I feel at ease and
   uncomfortable about   comfortable when
   interacting with them   interacting with them

   |___|___|___|___|___|___|___|___|___|___|

   I avoid contact of any sort because   I treat them just like
   I don't know how best to respond   anyone else

3. In the classroom I see children with special educational needs (SEN) as . . .

   |___|___|___|___|___|___|___|___|___|___|

   being a problem that I   being an asset that
   will have to cope with   will assist me

4. I know I will be working with children with SEN during my training/in my NQT year. I feel . . .

   |___|___|___|___|___|___|___|___|___|___|

   anxious/lacking in confidence   confident that I will
   about managing this aspect   manage this aspect of my
   of my placement   placement effectively

5. If I have to work with children who have the following needs I would feel . . .

   Difficulties with reading, writing or spelling

   |___|___|___|___|___|___|___|___|___|___|

   anxious/lacking in confidence   confident I could cope

   Behavioural difficulties

   |___|___|___|___|___|___|___|___|___|___|

   anxious/lacking in confidence   confident I could cope

   Physical difficulties

   |___|___|___|___|___|___|___|___|___|___|

   anxious/lacking in confidence   confident I could cope

   Gifted or talented

   |___|___|___|___|___|___|___|___|___|___|

   anxious/lacking in confidence   confident I could cope

   Hearing or visual impairments

   |___|___|___|___|___|___|___|___|___|___|

   anxious/lacking in confidence   confident I could cope

   English is not their first language

   |___|___|___|___|___|___|___|___|___|___|

   anxious/lacking in confidence   confident I could cope

Figure 1.1   Personal audit – attitudes and feelings about special needs

Children have special educational needs if they have a *learning difficulty* which calls for special educational provision to be made for them.

Children have a *learning difficulty* if they:

(a) have a significantly greater difficulty in learning than the majority of children of the same age; or

(b) have a disability which prevents or hinders them from making use of educational facilities of a kind generally provided for children of the same age in schools within the area of the local education authority; or

(c) are under compulsory school age and fall within the definition (a) or (b) above or would do so if *special educational provision* was not made for them.

Children must not be regarded as having a learning difficulty solely because the language or form of language of their home is different from the language in which they will be taught.

Special educational provision means:

(a) for children of 2 or over, educational provision which is additional to, or otherwise different from, the educational provision made generally for children of their age in schools maintained by the LEA, other than special schools, in the area; or

(b) for children under 2, educational provision of any kind.

(Education Act 1996, section 312)

Figure 1.2   The legal definition of special educational needs

The legal definition of special educational needs

The legal definition is contained in the Education Acts of 1981, 1993 and 1996. This definition excludes the needs of some children who you personally may consider also have special educational needs, e.g. the gifted and talented or children for whom English is a second language (EAL). The Act makes it clear that children for whom English is an additional language should not be considered as having special educational needs for this reason alone, although some children with EAL may, of course, have learning difficulties as well. The needs of children with EAL – those who are gifted and talented and other children who have particular needs – will be considered further in Chapter 3.

When reading the legal definition of special educational needs, what strikes you? Does it help you to understand better what a special educational need might be? Or are you feeling unsure as to what the definition is really saying? What, for example, does the phrase 'significantly greater' really mean? How significant does 'significant' have to be?

Take a few minutes to write down what queries and questions you still have about this definition and where you would like some clarification. Look back at this list from time to time and consider how your reading and further experience contributes to your understanding of the concept of special educational needs and the legal definition.

Historical context

We will be coming back to the definition, but before we do so let us briefly look at the history of special educational needs in England. The history of special education is fascinating in its own right, mirroring as it does the history of social welfare. However, it also provides us with a context when exploring issues relating to special educational needs as well as giving insights into the changing attitudes and needs of the society in which we live. As you read through this brief historical overview you might like to consider not only how attitudes have changed but also why they have changed.

The Forster Act (1870) to the 1944 Education Act

The Forster Act of 1870 marked the beginning of state provision for elementary education for most children. The availability of elementary education had, up until this time, been dependent upon the voluntary sector and, as such, was geograph-ically patchy. The Act established school boards to provide elementary education where there were insufficient places in voluntary schools. It sought to ensure a proper coverage so that all children could receive a basic education regardless of where they lived. The new school boards were able to provide for disabled pupils if they wished, but while some did, many did not. Thus the historical equivalent of a postcode lottery remained for many disabled children, with some receiving elementary education while others did not. This haphazard education system was affecting many children with a variety of educational needs long before the Forster Act but the Act did nothing to rescue this situation. Significant numbers of children with a variety of needs and difficulties remained outside the education system and this was to be the case for another hundred years.

Can you make an educated guess as to which disabilities were most likely to have been catered for by the newly established school boards?

Although hardly any school boards made specific provision for disabled pupils, a few did, notably for the deaf and the blind. It was not until the Education Act of 1893 that deaf and blind children in England received elementary education as of right. Provision for the physically and mentally disabled was to come even more slowly, and the most severely handicapped were largely cared for in a range of institutions rather than being educated. However, increasing numbers of children of below-average intellectual ability began to attend elementary schools with the implementation of the Forster Act and it soon became apparent that many of their needs were not being met.

The Royal Commission on the Blind and the Deaf (1889) contributed to the discussion about provision for the mentally handicapped and suggested three categories. 'Defectives' were the feeble-minded, imbeciles or idiots. The last were the most severely handicapped and were considered to be ineducable. It was recommended that imbeciles be taught by ordinary teachers while 'auxiliary' schools should be set up for the feeble-minded who were considered to need a special education. The physically handicapped were also classed as 'defective' by the Commission. Although the Commission's report was favourably received, the Elementary Education (Defective and Epileptic Children) Act of 1899 merely allowed school boards to make provision for the mentally and physically handicapped rather than requiring them to do so. It was not until the Elementary Education Act of 1914 that school boards were required to make provision for the mentally handicapped, and in 1918 the same requirement was made in respect of the physically defective and epileptic.

A further group of 'difficult to teach' children, later to be labelled as 'maladjusted', was also identified during this period. Some pioneering provision was made, including the advent of child guidance clinics, but this was largely at the instigation of medical services. Comparatively little provision was made by education authorities before 1944.

The 1944 Education Act – the postwar education system

The 1944 Education Act marked the beginning of the postwar education system and, as such, was far-reaching. As a result of the Act, LEAs now had a duty to identify which children required special educational treatment, could require children to be presented by their parents for medical examination and were responsible for ensuring that the needs of these children were met.

Categories of disability

Children had been, and remained, categorised, in medical terms, on the basis that if a diagnosis was made an educational 'treatment' could be prescribed. It was what is often referred to as a 'medical model'. The Handicapped Pupils and School Health Service Regulations of 1945 prescribed 11 categories of pupils: blind, partially sighted, deaf, partially deaf, delicate, diabetic, educationally subnormal (ESN), epileptic, maladjusted, physically handicapped and those with speech defects. These categories remained intact with the exception of diabetic, which became part of the delicate category in 1953. The regulations assumed that the blind, deaf, epileptic, physically handicapped and those with speech defects were severely disabled and should therefore be educated in special schools while the other children could attend ordinary schools if adequate provision could be made.

While there was a clear emphasis upon the avoidance of segregating children with difficulties wherever possible, the fact remained that many were segregated and labelled. The expansion of special schools was considerable during the next decade although the number of places needed for the ESN children and the maladjusted far outweighed those available during this period.

The modern era

The modern era of special education could be said to have begun with the Education (Handicapped Children) Act 1970. Up until the implementation of this Act, some children were still not considered educable and were therefore not entitled to an education. Most of these children had profound difficulties or disabilities and were cared for in hospitals, residential homes or at home. The Act entitled all children, regardless of difficulty or disability, to an education and, as a direct result, LEAs opened more special schools. The teachers working in the special schools received additional training.

The Warnock Report

The next significant milestone was the Warnock Report of 1978. The 1981 Education Act was based on many of the ideas from the Warnock Report, including the concept of special educational needs. The report recommended the dropping of the categories of difficulty such as the ESN and maladjusted in favour of the idea of a continuum of need and a focus on the individual child. To give a very simple example, by asking a question about general educational needs, if in your class there are two children who wear spectacles, would they have the same educational needs? One may be lively and articulate while the other may be shy and withdrawn. One may like to have background music on while reading; the other may prefer quiet for this activity. One may enjoy working as part of a team while the other may prefer to work alone, and so on. The fact that they both have a minor sight problem which is corrected by the wearing of spectacles does not give you, as a teacher, any real understanding or information as to how best a child might learn and how you can make your teaching more effective for that child. Both children in this example have very different educational needs.

If we now relate this to special educational needs, we could expand this illustration and ask if two children with a hearing impairment or similarly severe difficulties with spelling have the same special educational needs as each other? The Warnock focus opened the door to enabling the individual needs of a child to be identified, assessed and provided for. It recognised that each child is different and that categorising children when it came to making educational provision for them could be counter-productive and unhelpful.

The concept of special educational needs

One of the main suggestions of the Warnock Report was the acceptance of the idea of a continuum of need. It was recognised that children did not fit into labelled boxes but the range of special educational needs encompassed the severe to the mild, with everything in between. Thus child A may have a particular, relatively short-term, difficulty while child B may have a long-term difficulty which is more complex. The response to the needs of these children will be very different in spite of the fact that both may have, for example, difficulties associated with reading. Child A may have a difficulty with blending sounds together and may be slower at picking this skill up than some other children in the class. Child B may have severe learning and emotional difficulties and may also have difficulty in blending sounds.

The Warnock Report suggested that one in five children would be likely to have special educational needs at some time during their school career. Of this 20 per cent, the committee suggested that 2 per cent would have to have more severe or complex needs that, for some children, would require special school provision. However, it was also envisaged that a significant number of the 2 per cent would be educated in mainstream schools. The report recommended the issuing of statements in order to ensure that these children received the provision they need. This was implemented in the 1981 Education Act and more information about this can be found in Chapter 2.

The Warnock focus on individual needs included issues such as access to the curriculum, modification to the curriculum when appropriate and attention to the learning environment. While there were, and are, those who did not feel that the report went far enough, for many these ideas represented a radical rethink. Needs and abilities became the focus instead of the disability or medical label.

Other recommendations

The Warnock Report also made recommendations about:

- partnership with parents;
- the curriculum;
- the transition from schooling to adult life;
- the role of support and advisory services and other professionals, e.g. social workers, health services;
- the place of integration; and
- teacher education.

The report recommended that there should be a range of provision to include mainstream with support, special schools, units attached to mainstream schools and, where appropriate, education at home. Integration, often considered the forerunner of inclusion, featured strongly with three levels being identified. The first was *locational* integration, where a child with SEN would be educated in, for example, a unit in the same location as a mainstream school. If the child spent some time with children in the mainstream setting, for example play times or lunchtimes, this was known as *social* integration, which was a step up from purely locational integration. *Functional* integration was when a child with SEN worked alongside children in a mainstream classroom.

As already indicated, the 1981 Act was largely based on the Warnock Report. A significant part of the Act was the identification and assessment of SEN and the responsibilities for the statementing of children at the most severe end of the SEN continuum. The most significant pieces of legislation relating to SEN since then have been:

- the Education Reform Act of 1988, which introduced the National Curriculum;
- the Children Act (1989), which covered issues of Child Protection and 'looked-after' children;
- the Disability Discrimination Act (1995);
- the Education Act (1996);
- the Special Educational Needs and Disability Act (2001); and
- the Children Act (2004), which covers all services that are accessed by children including those with additional needs.

The 'Every Child Matters' programme supports the implementation of the Children Act 2004 and is wide-ranging. It includes guidance for education, health and social services. The programme website (see 'Where to find further information') gives full coverage of all the many aspects of this agenda including downloadable documents and a timeline for the implementation of different elements of the programme. The QtT and HLTA standards were published before the 2004 Children Act and the implementation of the Every Child Matters programme, and therefore do not refer specifically to either of these. However, since many children with SEN and other educational needs make considerable use of a range of children's services, it is in your interests to be familiar with this programme and to think about how the Code of Practice relates to it.

Legislation and the revised SEN Code of Practice (2001)

The Code of Practice on the Identification and Assessment of Special Educational Needs (DFE 1994) came into effect as a result of the Education Act of 1993. The rights and duties in the 1993 Act were consolidated into the 1996 Education Act and new duties were introduced by the Special Educational Needs and Disability Act of 2001. The revised SEN Code of Practice (2001) takes these into account as well as feedback from the consultation carried out on the proposed revisions. The next chapter looks at the SEN Code of Practice in more detail.

REFLECTION POINTS

1. Terms such as 'defectives', 'imbeciles' and 'the feeble-minded' were in frequent use when the Forster Act 1870 came into being. What is your reaction to them? What terms have you heard or seen recently that you would consider to be unacceptable today?

2. To what extent are labels helpful to the classroom teacher, parents, teaching assistants and trainee teachers? As a starting point you might like to suggest labels that are current and then consider these and/or the following:

   (a) dyslexic

   (b) autistic

   (c) 'clumsy'

   (d) 'has cerebral palsy'

   How much do these labels tell you about the child and his/her strengths, weaknesses and needs? Could you plan for this child on the basis of these labels? If not, what else would you need to know? Are there any circumstances in which these labels might actually be unhelpful?

3. In what ways do you think the attitude of the general public to disability has changed since the Warnock Committee reported in 1978 and what do you think the reasons for this are?

CHAPTER 2

The SEN Code of Practice

Standards S2.6 (QTS) and 2.8 (HLTA) relate specifically to knowledge of and familiarity with the SEN Code of Practice. This chapter looks at the purpose, content and impact of the Code as well as the responsibilities of a class or subject teacher that the Code describes. Although the Code of Practice applies solely to settings in England, all teachers will benefit from consideration of its principles and guidance for good practice.

The purpose of the SEN Code of Practice

The revised SEN Code of Practice (DfES 2001b) has been effective since 1 January 2002 and, in England, replaces the original 1994 Code. Its purpose, similar to the original, is 'to give practical guidance' and advice to LEAs, governing bodies of state schools and government funded Early Years settings and to all who help them (e.g. health and social services) to meet their responsibilities for children and young people with special educational needs. It is a statutory requirement that all these bodies must take into account what the Code says when making decisions. However, the Code does not prescribe what should happen in individual cases.

The original Code of Practice sought to embed good practice with regard to the identification and assessment of special educational needs. It emphasised the fact that class and subject teachers were expected to be able to meet the needs of all children in their class, including those with SEN, and not to think that those children were someone else's responsibility. It was based on the recommendations of the Warnock Report (DES 1978), was in keeping with the concept of a continuum of need and took a staged approach to the identification and assessment of special educational needs.

The graduated response of the SEN Code of Practice (2001)

In the SEN Code of Practice, the staged approach of the 1994 Code has become a 'graduated response' with an emphasis on action which is in addition to or different from the differentiated curriculum normally provided. In other words, action needs to be taken because the normal differentiated curriculum is not meeting the child's needs and he/she is not making adequate progress in spite of this differentiation.

The first action is taken by the class or subject teacher and/or member of the pastoral team with the support of the special educational needs co-ordinator

THE FIVE CORE PRINCIPLES OF THE CODE OF PRACTICE

The Code is based upon five core principles which can be found in section 1:5 under 'Fundamental principles':

- A child with special educational needs should have their needs met
- The special educational needs of children will normally be met in mainstream schools or settings
- The views of the child should be sought and taken into account
- Parents have a vital role to play in supporting their child's education
- Children with special educational needs should be offered full access to a broad, balanced and relevant education, including an appropriate curriculum for the foundation stage and the National Curriculum

(DfES 2001b, section 1:5)

THE CONTENTS OF THE CODE OF PRACTICE AND HOW IT IS PRESENTED

There are ten sections plus annexes of regulations and a glossary. Each section and paragraph is numbered so, for example, 3:18 refers to section 3, paragraph 18.

Section 1: 'Principles and policies' sets out the context for the Code and the principles and legislation on which it is based.

Section 2 is about partnership with parents.

Section 3 considers pupil participation.

Sections 4 to 6 cover identification, assessment and provision in Early Years, primary and secondary phases respectively.

Sections 7 to 9 are concerned with statutory assessment, statementing and annual reviews.

Section 10 covers working with other agencies.

Figure 2.1 The SEN Code of Practice

(SENCO), and the child/young person would usually have an Individual Education Plan (IEP) (see below). If this action is not sufficient to enable the child to make progress, the child can be moved to Action Plus when he/she will be referred to an outside agency such as the LEA support services. A new IEP will usually be drawn up. Table 2.1 shows the main features of the graduated response.

Statutory assessment and statementing

There will be a small number of children for whom provision at School Action Plus or Early Years Action Plus is inadequate. This group equates to 'the Warnock 2 per cent'. In these circumstances it may be appropriate to consider if the child should be formally assessed and a statement of special educational need issued. A statement is a legal document which determines the special educational provision for a child or where the resources normally available are insufficient or

Table 2.1 The graduated response model (SEN Code of Practice)

	What is involved	Who is involved
Early Years Action (EYA)	Action additional to or different from that provided in the normal differentiated curriculum. An IEP	Early Years Practitioner (EYP) and SENCO
Early Years Action Plus (EYA+)	Action additional to or different from that provided in Early Years Action. An IEP	SENCO takes lead responsibility, EYP has day-to-day responsibility and outside agencies are involved.
School Action (SA)	Action additional to or different from that provided in the normal differentiated curriculum. An IEP	Class teacher/subject teacher and/or member of the pastoral team and SENCO
School Action Plus (SA+)	Action additional to or different from that provided in School Action. An IEP	SENCO takes lead responsibility, class or subject teacher has day-to-day responsibility and outside agencies are involved.
Statutory assessment	Request made to LEA by head teacher, parents or services such as health. LEA decides if there is a need. If there is, assessment carried out and advice sought.	
Statement of SEN	Drawn up if LEA decides advice given warrants this.	

inappropriate to meet his/her needs. The head teacher, an agency such as a health service or social services or parents may request statutory assessment. Section 7 of the Code of Practice details the process involved.

Role of the LEA

The LEA first considers if there is a need for a statutory assessment by working with the school, the parents and outside agencies. If the LEA decides that it is necessary, an assessment is carried out and the LEA must request written parental, educational, medical, psychological and social services advice together with advice from other sources as appropriate. When all the advice is gathered, the LEA decides whether or not to draw up a statement of special educational needs. If the decision is taken not to issue a statement, the parents and school are given reasons for this decision. There are clear time-frames for all stages of the statutory assessment and statementing processes. A statement is reviewed at least annually so that any changes can be made as appropriate. Further details can be found in section 9 of the Code.

There are six sections to a statement. These are prescribed in the regulations in Annex A of the Code and further detail is to be found in section 8.

- Part 1 gives details such as the child's name, date of birth etc.
- Part 2 describes all the child's special educational needs as identified during statutory assessment.
- Part 3 contains details of the special educational provision that the LEA will make to meet the child's needs.
- Part 4 identifies the educational placement.
- Part 5 sets out any other needs that are not educational, e.g. health needs.
- Part 6 identifies non-educational provision.

All the advice given during statutory assessment is attached to the statement.

Individual Education Plans (IEPs)

An IEP is a record of the action to be taken in order to enable a child to make progress. The Code refers to it in the glossary (p. 203) as a 'planning, teaching and reviewing tool'. Group Education Plans (GEPs) are drawn up where several children in the class have common targets for which common strategies are appropriate.

The plans should include:

- targets
- strategies to be used
- names of people involved
- a review date
- success criteria
- outcomes

An IEP or GEP should therefore always state what is to be done, by whom and when. IEPs and GEPs will be extremely important for you when on school placements. Their existence should ensure that the children who have them will make progress and that you are informed and supported in your part in their implementation. Do ask to see them.

It is important to appreciate that an IEP should be concerned with strategies that are over and above normal differentiation in the class, rather than being a means of documenting and recording what should be occurring anyway. Specific guidance can be found in the SEN Code of Practice at 4:27–4:28 for Early Years, 5:50–5:53 for the primary phase and 6:58–6:60 for secondary.

The pupil

Section 3 of the Code covers issues relating to pupil participation and begins with a statement relating to articles 12 and 13 of the United Nations Convention on the Rights of the Child. It makes it clear that children and young people who are 'capable of forming views' have the right to participate in making decisions about matters which affect them. The Code makes it equally clear that a child's involvement is not just in relation to SEN; pupil participation should be the goal for all children (3:9).

Parents/carers

The Warnock Report effectively made the first step towards involving parents in their child's special education and in establishing the principle of professionals working in partnership with parents. Whenever you see the term 'parents' you need to remember that this includes any who have parental responsibility, e.g. foster carers, the local authority if a child is 'looked after', etc. This is clearly laid out in paragraphs 2:4 and 2:5.

Partnership with parents is one of the guiding principles in the SEN Code of Practice. Parents should be informed and involved at all stages so there should never be a situation where parents are unaware that their child is experiencing difficulties.

Parental partnership services are funded by every LEA and provided either by the LEA itself or by a voluntary organisation. Where the service is provided by the LEA, steps will always have been taken to enable parents to have confidence in the neutrality of the advice, support and information given. This is a very important element of the service as there will be times when parents wish to make representations to the LEA or there is a difference of opinion about a child's needs or SEN provision.

Parents do have recourse to the SEN Tribunal if they disagree with any element of a proposed statement or changes to an existing one, but this should be as a last resort. In most cases, the parent partnership service can assist in avoiding conflict.

The class or subject teacher

Early identification of a child's needs is very important. A few children will start school having had an IEP as part of Early Years Action (EYA) or Action Plus (EYA+). For others, baseline assessment soon after the child starts school will identify possible SEN. For others, their special educational needs may only become apparent after a period of time. In all cases, assessment should be a continual process. The class or subject teacher should report any concerns to the head teacher and/or the SENCO, keep appropriate records of progress and, of course, keep parents informed and involved.

The SENCO

The role of the SENCO is described in section 4 for Early Years settings, section 5 for primary schools and section 6 for secondary (4:15–4:17, 5:30–5:32, 6:32–6:35). The SENCO has a key role in the management of SEN provision in a school or Early Years setting and generally takes responsibility for the day-to-day management of this. Other responsibilities include liaison with colleagues in the school, parents and outside agencies and the general co-ordination of SEN provision in the school. The Code also includes sections (e.g. 5:33–5:36) about the time given to SENCOs to fulfil their role appropriately.

The school governors

The roles and duties of the governing body and the SEN governor are discussed in paragraphs 1:21 and 1:22 in section 1. All other references to governing bodies can be found in the index.

Support services and outside agencies

Every LEA has its own support services but how these are organised and managed varies considerably as does their size and scope. The minimum is an educational psychology service plus the services of teachers for children with sensory impairments. Many LEAs, however, have larger support services than this which may include learning, behavioural, other support teachers (supporting children for whom English is an additional language, and travellers), education social workers, specialist Educational Psychologists (EPs) etc. Every maintained school is required to publish information about their arrangements for working with support services and other outside agencies so this is a good source of information when you are on school placements. Procedures for referral of children to support services will vary but all local authorities will have guidelines or criteria for referrals.

Voluntary and other outside agencies may also provide services for teachers or parents and sometimes have provision as well, e.g. special schools or additional teaching facilities.

Other services such as health and social services may have a prominent role to play in meeting a child's needs. You will have noticed that social services and medical advice must be sought by the LEA as part of the statutory assessment procedures and there are references to these services throughout the Code. The guiding principle is that all services should work together closely in the best interests of the child and his/her family. You will undoubtedly have children in your class at some point with whom a number of outside agencies are involved.

From the example in Figure 2.2 it is easy to see how important it is that the services involved work together and with the family in as coherent a way as possible. In such complex circumstances, Anne could easily be receiving conflicting advice from the professionals involved as each will undoubtedly have his/her

---

Anne is a single parent with three children – Charlie, Karen and David. Anne is supported by social services and, at one point when she was in financial difficulties and very depressed, all three children were on the 'at risk' register. The children each have their own social worker from social services.

Charlie is in Year 9 at the local secondary school, has learning and behavioural difficulties and is statemented. The LEA's learning support service is involved and a support teacher works closely with the school's SENCO and Charlie's learning mentor (LM). A behavioural support teacher visits Charlie in school twice a month and also supports his teachers and LM. The educational psychologist reviews Charlie's progress twice a year and attends his annual review along with the support service teachers and colleagues from social services.

Karen is in Year 5 at the local primary school. She also has learning difficulties but is making good progress under Action Plus and is supported by an SEN teaching assistant in her class, along with two other children.

David is in Year 3 and attends the same primary school as Karen. He has muscular dystrophy and uses a wheelchair. In addition to the medical services involved, the support teacher for children with physical difficulties advises school and Anne.

Figure 2.2   Case study – Charlie (Y9), Karen (Y5) and David (Y3)

particular priorities. Unless there is co-operation between the various services the family could find it more difficult, rather than easier, to cope.

The majority of the children and young people with SEN in your classes will be at Action or Action Plus. When you have a child with more complex difficulties and needs in your class, it is likely that he/she will have a statement and you will usually find that there is advice and support for teachers available from the support services and other outside agencies. In the next chapter we will consider the range of needs that children with SEN may have.

REFLECTION POINTS

The following suggestions may help you to gain greater insight into the way schools implement the Code.

1. Collect any examples of IEP or GEP proformas and consider how user-friendly they are for teachers, pupils, teaching assistants, parents and trainee teachers (see Appendix B for further examples).

2. Whenever you have the opportunity, discuss specific IEPs with the teachers involved and find out what they would consider to be normal differentiation and how the IEP strategies differ from this.

3. Read the introduction to section 3, 'Pupil participation', together with paragraphs 3:1–3:3. Make notes of examples of effective practice you hear or read about. Make a point of asking teachers and SENCOs about practice in your school or placement school(s).

4. Talk to your SENCO about his/her role in school and how it has developed.

The range of needs

This chapter is a very basic starting point and aims to provide you with further avenues of enquiry. Bear in mind, as already discussed, that the educational needs of children and young people do not fall into neat boxes or categories. Although needs have been grouped for the purposes of this introduction, the needs of many learners will span more than one group. The range of difficulties resulting from a particular disorder may also span more than one group, e.g. autism may result in communication, language, global learning and behavioural difficulties for one child while for another child, with less severe autism, needs may relate mostly to communication.

The class or subject teacher's role

The role of the class or subject teacher, in relation to special educational needs, as described in the Code of Practice, is discussed in Chapter 2. If you are an NQT you will clearly not have the experience of those who have been teaching for longer, but you are expected to be able to seek out advice, information and support in order to meet the educational needs of all your pupils.

Induction
Standard b

You will obviously not be expected to know everything, but you are expected to take responsibility to seek support as necessary. There are many ways in which you can access support, but your first port of call will be other teachers in the school and, particularly where SEN is concerned, the SENCO. LEA and other support services will be available to assist, particularly in the case of the more complex, severe or less common needs, e.g. sensory or physical difficulties. There are many organisations and groups that are able to provide information and, of course, the parent/carer and the child him/herself are extremely important sources of information and guidance. The resources section at the end of the book gives contact details of organisations and institutions that may be of help to you, together with details of books, websites, etc. These are listed by topic.

The range of needs

Induction
Standards b
and c

I have, for ease, grouped a variety of needs and difficulties together under the following headings:

- Communication difficulties
- Behavioural, emotional and social difficulties

- Specific learning difficulties, e.g. dyspraxia, dyslexia
- General or global learning difficulties
- Sensory impairment
- Physical difficulties and medical conditions

Some broad observations and comments about each area of need will be given, but please bear in mind that each child is an individual with his/her own pattern of strengths, difficulties and needs. What follows can only be, at best, a very broad and general overview.

Communication difficulties

Many children with SEN will experience some degree of difficulty with communication. When considering the range of SEN, it is probably helpful to first think about communication in general. Communication is a two-way process. A message from one source has to be correctly understood by another for effective communication to have taken place. If the message is not delivered in a way which can be understood by the receiver, a successful interaction will not have taken place. In order for communication to take place, a message sender needs to have:

- something to communicate;
- a means of communication; and
- a reason to communicate.

The second point, a means of communication, is possibly the easiest to consider first. Communication can obviously only take place if the child has access to a way of making a message understandable to and by others. Much of the communication in school is through speech and written language, although there are, of course, other ways of communicating including gestures and signs (e.g. sign language), diagrams/drawings etc. and combinations of methods. If a child has difficulties with writing, reading and/or recording learning, this has the potential to impede progress in learning. Similarly, early speech and oral language difficulties can, in their turn, impede learning to read at a later stage.

The first and third points were 'something to communicate' and 'a reason to communicate'. We communicate because we want or need to for some reason. Some children, e.g. those with severe autism, may only seldom seek to interact with others at all and may not have the language or the understanding to do so. Communication difficulties are therefore likely to be a major area of need for them.

In terms of the receipt of the communicated message, access to a means of communication is vital, together with the ability to understand and interpret the message accurately. The message may otherwise not be received at all, or not received as intended.

Speech and language difficulties

The terms 'language delay' and 'language disorder' are both in common usage but sometimes one is used when the other is meant, which can cause confusion.

Language disorder usually means that the development of a child's language is not following the 'normal' pattern. Language delay, on the other hand, refers to language development which *does* follow the 'normal' pattern but is that of a younger child. It is probably more helpful to describe a child's language skills than run the risk of using terminology that will have different meanings for different people.

For some children communication difficulties will be specifically related to speech and/or language. The means of communication will be affected or impaired in some way, e.g. a physical difficulty in actually producing sounds (utterances). Another child may have a difficulty in making the connections needed to understand language and therefore not be able to use it effectively as a means of communication.

There is a range of language difficulties including expressive, pragmatic, listening and comprehension difficulties, each of which is briefly referred to below. Speech and language therapists, usually working in the health services, can offer more specialised support and help to teachers. However, you should be aware that, in some areas, these colleagues are in relatively short supply and waiting lists can be lengthy.

Expressive language difficulties

These are difficulties with the production and expression of language, e.g. sounds, words and/or grammar. The child may, for example, only be able to physically produce a limited number of sounds and may also substitute some sounds for others. This will result in an individual pattern of speech which others may not be able to understand until or unless they 'tune in' to the particular pattern.

Possible causes of such difficulties might include:

- a physical problem with facial muscles;
- a hearing impairment where a child cannot hear certain frequencies and therefore some sounds;
- lack of experience of the meaning of words (e.g. through having a limited exposure to a range of language);
- poor memory for words or poor linking skills (so words may not be put together in a meaningful way); and
- difficulties with grammatical understanding.

Pragmatic difficulties

These are difficulties in using language appropriately, e.g. in maintaining conversation, responding appropriately, inferring (i.e. extracting the meaning) appropriately etc. A child with such difficulties *may* appear to be able to read and also to speak very well.

Listening or attention difficulties

There can be a number of causes for these difficulties including:

- hearing loss
- pragmatic difficulties
- poor language comprehension
- poor auditory memory (e.g. for sounds, words or phrases)
- anxiety

Comprehension difficulties

A child may have a poor understanding of written and/or spoken language; he/she may appear to read well but may not understand the meaning of what has been read. Similar communication difficulties may be present with the spoken word. For some children, the difficulties relate to having a purpose, or reason, for communicating. Autistic Spectrum Disorder is a good example.

Autistic Spectrum Disorder (ASD)

For a child to be diagnosed as having ASD, three specific areas of difficulty must be present. These are known as the 'triad of impairment'. The triad can be summarised as:

- Social – little or no attention to responses of others; rarely initiates interaction with others;
- Language and communication – difficulty in understanding non-verbal communication, e.g. gestures, body language, uses language literally, finds it difficult to talk about feelings;
- Thought and behaviour – unable to play imaginatively, misses the point of conversations, tends to focus on very specific items/issues rather than having an overview.

Children with ASD usually display repetitive behaviours. Routines are very important and they tend not to like any changes to their normal routine. Sometimes they have very challenging behaviours, e.g. screaming, biting. As with all areas of difficulty there are degrees of severity, and ASD can also occur with other conditions such as cerebral palsy, dyslexia etc.

About 10 per cent of children with ASD have a special skill. This is most usually in the fields of art, music or numeric calculation, and you may have seen examples of this in the media. Seventy-five per cent of children with ASD have some degree of learning difficulty.

Asperger's syndrome is part of the ASD continuum. Children with Asperger's are generally of average or above-average intelligence and often have a high level of verbal behaviour. They will usually initiate and want contact with others although they will not always 'read' body language or responses. They also tend to have obsessional interests rather than performing repetitive physical actions. A significant number also have dyspraxic tendencies (see 'Dyspraxia' in the 'Specific learning difficulties' section below).

As you will appreciate from the overview of Autistic Spectrum Disorder above, children with more severe forms are likely to display challenging behaviours in the classroom. This is a good illustration of the fact that individual needs can span a range of different areas of difficulty and that the pre-Warnock categories could not adequately define a child's educational needs.

Behavioural, emotional and social difficulties

Of all the areas of special educational need these are probably both the most emotive and the most difficult to define. At what point, for example, does unacceptable behaviour becomes a special educational need? All children (and adults) are naughty sometimes, after all. However, most children respond positively to correction, even if they do need telling more than once. The significant factors are:

- the severity of the behaviour;
- its frequency;
- the context in which it occurs; and
- the age/stage of development of the child.

As an example, a two-year-old throwing a tantrum at the supermarket checkout because his parent would not allow him to have the sweets he could see might be considered usual behaviour for a child of that age in the circumstances. However, as a child becomes older, such behaviour becomes less usual and there comes a point where it would be regarded as inappropriate and of concern. The whole question becomes even more complex, however, when you consider that what individuals see as normal, acceptable behaviour in the particular circumstances is highly variable. What one teacher or parent might tolerate another would not. Context plays a very significant part in behaviour, and altering the context can make a difference to the behaviour (which is why some supermarkets have sweet-free checkouts). What is important is the recognition that, when a child does have behavioural, emotional or social difficulties, he/she is likely to be under stress and not in full control of his/her actions.

When you think about inappropriate behaviour I would guess that your first thoughts are likely to be of behaviour which is unwanted, challenging and disruptive. This may be relatively low level, e.g. shouting out, fidgeting, inattention, or more serious, e.g. bullying, swearing or physical or verbal aggression. You will probably be anxious about your ability to deal with this and this anxiety in itself can create a vicious circle because it may well be communicated to the children and signal your insecurity. Further chapters (6 and 7 in particular) will address this and related issues.

Other children may display 'acting in' behaviours, e.g. by becoming very withdrawn, appearing to be in their own world or depressed, just sitting quietly but doing nothing, not speaking, not interacting with other children or adults etc. This may be perceived as easier to deal with than more challenging behaviour as the child is not disrupting the rest of the class or the teacher in the same way as a child who is acting out. However, this also makes it potentially easier not take positive action as quickly as would be desirable.

The cause of unwanted behaviours, whether acting out or in, are many and include:

- specific disorders with a physical cause (e.g. ADHD, see below);
- as a consequence of other needs, e.g. a gifted child not being stretched enough or a child with EAL struggling with written language demands;
- as a consequence of other difficulties (e.g. the frustration that may be experienced by a child with dyslexia);
- medication or treatment;
- poor role models or disadvantageous circumstances at home;
- inappropriate teaching approaches or curriculum;
- not having learnt appropriate behaviour; and
- poor self-esteem.

Attention Deficit (Hyperactivity) Disorder

I have specifically included this disorder, not only because it is more commonly recognised now than in the past but also because it is highly likely that you will teach children who either do have the disorder or who are labelled as such. A few years ago, when ADHD was much in the media, there appeared a number of 'checklists' in magazines so that parents could see if their child had the condition. The problem with such checklists is that most of us display some of the characteristics, albeit in a mild form. It is much more useful if you can objectively describe what the child does and in what circumstances, what he/she can and can't do. This is not only more likely to be of help to other professionals in making an accurate diagnosis, where appropriate, but will also give you a great deal more information about what strategies to use to meet the child's needs. This is discussed further in Chapter 4.

The prime characteristics of ADD are:

- poor attention span
- poor short-term memory

ADHD has the same characteristics but with the addition of:

- a low frustration threshold
- heightened activity, impulsiveness and inflexibility

Children with these disorders do not choose to be disobedient, but the evidence is that they have a chemical imbalance in the brain. As with Autistic Spectrum Disorder, ADHD is also a spectrum disorder with a range of levels of difficulty experienced, from very mild to severe.

Behaviour modification strategies and/or medical intervention with drugs remain the approaches most commonly used to deal with the aspects of ADHD that interfere most with a normal life such as low frustration threshold and impulsiveness. A behaviour modification programme requires a series of steps that include:

- the identification of the behaviour that is to be encouraged;
- the rewards (or punishment) to be given if the behaviour does (or does not) occur;

- a contract between the child and teacher/parent; and
- the implementation and evaluation of the programme.

Drugs such as Ritalin have been used quite extensively to reduce the level of activity, impulsiveness etc., but it can be difficult to get the correct dose and they do have side-effects. A new generation of drugs is now coming into use with fewer side-effects.

Attention-seeking behaviours

It can be easy to think that a child who is trying and seeks attention frequently has ADHD, but there is a significant difference between attention-seeking and ADHD. A child who is attention-seeking may be extremely demanding of a teacher's time and attention, but will usually be able to work with the teacher on a one-to-one basis. A child with ADHD will usually have problems with paying attention even when working on a one-to-one basis.

Social difficulties

These relate specifically to a child's interactions with others, and the most obvious signs of difficulty are inappropriate responses to others in particular circumstances, again, in relation to the child's point of development. Most children learn how to respond appropriately in given situations but for some there are clear difficulties. These may relate to social isolation or responding aggressively in circumstances when other children would not. Low self-esteem is frequently present.

Specific learning difficulties

Some children have specific and significant difficulties with particular areas of learning. Most commonly, these are with reading, writing, spelling or number work. There is a mismatch between these areas of difficulty and the child's general level of ability and achievement so, for example, a child may have a reading age two years below his/her chronological age and yet be extremely articulate, having a high level of achievement in some subject areas. Frustration levels can be high and self-esteem and behaviour can suffer as a result.

Dorothy Smith (1996, p. 6) defines specific learning difficulties as being:

significant problems of synthesising (bringing together information in the brain), organising (making sense and order of this information) and memorising (holding on to this information in order to use it at will).

A child with specific learning difficulties will have problems in one or more of these three areas.

Dyslexia

The word dyslexia comes from the roots 'dys' meaning difficulty and 'lexia' meaning language. It is estimated by the British Dyslexia Association that 4 per cent of the population is severely dyslexic and that up to 10 per cent has some degree of difficulty. Dyslexia is therefore relatively common and you will almost inevitably teach dyslexic children during your career.

Dyslexia is congenital, i.e. people are born with it. It can run in families and it has a neurological basis. As a result of the problems indicated above, children with dyslexia will experience a range of difficulties in some but not necessarily all of the following areas:

- motor control;
- concentration span;
- organisation skills;
- sequencing skills (auditory and/or visual), e.g. following instructions, constructing text, sequencing events, sorting by shape;
- directional confusion, e.g. understanding directional language, reversing letters (e.g. b and d);
- language skills such as word-naming, mispronunciation, putting letters in the wrong order or leaving out some of a word, inferencing skills, poor sound blending. As a result of these the child will experience difficulties with reading, spelling and/or writing; and
- poor concept of time.

It should be noted that while some children with dyslexia experience considerable motor control difficulties, others excel in areas such as design and technology, sport and art and may have exceptional abilities in terms of spatial awareness. This serves to illustrate that the label 'dyslexia' can only be of limited help in determining what an individual child's educational needs might be.

Dyspraxia

The word dyspraxia comes from the roots 'dys' meaning difficulty and 'praxis' meaning doing. Children with dyspraxia have motor co-ordination problems which are not associated with any known neurological problem. It is an impairment of the organisation of movement. There is no set pattern but the child will experience difficulties in some of the following areas:

- fine motor control, e.g. handwriting difficulties, poor grip for utensils (e.g. eating);
- gross motor control difficulties, e.g. hopping and skipping, completing an obstacle course;
- articulation of speech (caused by physical co-ordination difficulties with facial muscles etc.);
- attention and concentration;
- organisational skills, e.g. forgetfulness, difficulty in adapting to routines and with dressing/undressing, organising thoughts, following instructions; and
- visual perceptual skills and visual motor skills, e.g. judging distance.

Portwood (2000) gives case studies and pen portaits of children with dyspraxia, information about the identification and assessment of children with dyspraxia and lots of classroom suggestions.

General or global learning difficulties (GLD)

Some children have general or global learning difficulties. These are present across the majority of the curriculum and there is not the mismatch between performance in different areas as is the case in specific learning difficulties. In broad general terms, children with global learning difficulties are likely to:

- have difficulty with basic literacy and numeracy skills; and

- need more time, practice and review to consolidate their learning than their peers.

They are significantly slower than their classmates, e.g. in starting and/or completing tasks. Some children with global learning difficulties are able to learn facts (e.g. times tables or the spelling of a particular word) and repeat them, but may have limited understanding of the meaning of what they have learnt or how to apply it.

Sensory impairment

Sensory difficulties include both visual and hearing impairments. There are many types of visual and hearing impairment and appropriate medical and classroom approaches will therefore differ accordingly. The specialist teacher will be able to advise you on the optimum working conditions for the child and on the educational implications of their particular difficulties. LEAs will have specialist teachers to support children with these difficulties. Should you have a child in your class with a significant sensory impairment, take the advice already given to the school by a specialist support teacher and/or seek further advice from him/her as necessary.

Remember that sensory impairments can be mild to severe and the impact upon the child's learning, behaviour and self-esteem will be variable. Equally, some children will have had the impairment from birth, while for others it will have come suddenly or over a period of time. For some, the condition will become worse over time while for others, medical advances, e.g. cochlear implants, may offer some improvement. The child's responses to offers of aids and adult support will vary as will their levels of self-esteem and ability to cope with the demands of the classroom.

A common cause of temporary and fluctuating moderate hearing loss in younger children is a condition known as 'glue ear', where the fluid in the middle ear thickens and affects hearing. You may find that a child doesn't respond when called, picks up only part of what has been said or confuses similar sounding words. At other times the child's hearing may be significantly better and it is during these times that good listening habits need to be established so that the child doesn't miss learning these important skills. Those working with the child can help by:

- gaining his/her attention before talking;
- providing the best possible listening conditions, e.g. placing the child close to the teacher and where there is the least background noise;

- providing breaks from listening; and
- providing the best conditions for lip-reading, i.e. keeping still while giving instructions, standing in a good light and where the child can see easily.

Adults in mainstream schools will also work with many pupils who have common eye defects such as long- or short-sightedness and who wear spectacles or contact lenses for these or other common conditions. For younger children in particular it will be important to know when spectacles should be worn and the extent to which they correct vision, as some eye conditions cannot be corrected to a normal level. Ensuring visual materials are of good quality (especially photocopies), with good contrast, and that the child is sitting in appropriate light conditions will assist.

Physical difficulties and medical conditions

The range of physical difficulties and medical conditions is vast and it is not the task of this book to try to list them all. However, there are some general issues to be considered including:

- implications for accessing the curriculum, for teaching, for learning and for support;
- practical implications for the child, teacher and other children and adults in school; and
- side-effects of medication, secondary effects, consequences, e.g. hospitalisation, emotional, social or behavioural difficulties or mental health problems.

The main question for the teacher to ask is how the medical condition and/or its treatment is likely to affect the individual child's performance in motor tasks and in progressive tasks. The answer will be different for each child but this provides a good starting point for the teacher in ascertaining how best to meet a child's particular needs.

Individual needs, as always, will vary according to the severity of the condition, individual strengths, weaknesses etc., but I am giving two examples of conditions to illustrate the possible impact on a child's performance at school. The first is epilepsy, 1. because it is one of the three most common medical conditions (the other two being asthma and diabetes), and 2. because it is a condition about which there remains more prejudice and misunderstanding than many others.

Epilepsy

As with all medical conditions and disabilities, some children are more severely affected than others but it is important to keep this in perspective and to remember that the majority of children with epilepsy live normal lives. The areas of learning that may be affected by epilepsy are:

- speed of processing information;
- recall, keeping focused and alert; and
- smoothness of motor movement and/or language.

27

There are two main types of seizure – generalised and partial. In the case of the former, the child will be unconscious at the onset and so will fall to the ground. The muscles relax and contract which results in jerky movement. Clearly, the most important thing is that the child does not hurt him/herself as a result of the seizure. A partial seizure may not result in a loss of consciousness but the child will lose a sense of his/her surroundings. This may be for no more than a moment or two. Many also have some degree of warning before a seizure occurs, but this is very individual.

Whenever a seizure, however minor, has taken place, brain activity is affected immediately after and, in more severe cases, for a longer period of time. A child, for example, who has nocturnal seizures may find difficulty in maintaining attention or processing information as quickly as usual well into the next day or beyond. For many children with epilepsy, drugs control their seizures, so unless their parents have informed school that they have epilepsy, you could be unaware.

Cerebral palsy

This condition is included because it is a broad term that covers a range of conditions characterised by some or all of the following:

- involuntary movements or spasms;
- muscle contraction that results in inflexibility and therefore movement problems;
- poor balance or co-ordination; and
- speech, hearing or visual impairments.

Clearly, the effects for an individual will vary enormously according to their combination and severity. While some will have learning difficulties, many will not and can be, potentially, high academic achievers. There are numerous practical aids available, e.g. key guards (to avoid keys being touched accidentally when using a computer); switches for accessing computers activated by different body parts such as the chin or head as appropriate; pencil grips; specialist sports equipment that is, for example, lighter or more easily gripped.

It is important to remember that the fact that a child may have a medical condition does not necessarily mean that the child has SEN. A medical diagnosis is not the same as an educational need. For some children it may be more a question of managing their medical condition rather than SEN provision being required. There can, for example, be few classrooms nowadays that do not contain a child with asthma who requires the use of an inhaler from time to time. This is not a special educational need any more than the wearing of glasses is for most people.

Severe, complex or profound difficulties

It is made clear in paragraph 7:52 (Code of Practice) that the guidance is not suggesting that there are *categories* of need. It does, however, suggest that the range of special educational needs can be organised into four main areas while also emphasising that the needs of an individual child may fall into more than one of these. The suggested areas of need are:

- communication and interaction;

- cognition and learning;

- behavioural, emotional and social development; and

- sensory and/or physical.

A child with autism and cerebral palsy together may, for example, have considerable needs in all four areas.

While the Code of Practice refers to different needs, e.g. general learning or behavioural difficulties at various points in the earlier chapters, it is section 7 that provides guidance about statutory assessment and therefore relates to more complex or severe difficulties and needs. The broad areas of need are considered in greater detail and guidance is provided as to both the nature of the difficulties and the range of provision that might need to be considered. The Code emphasises that if the suitable arrangements to meet the child's needs can be made at School Action Plus, a statement should not be provided. However, if such arrangements have been made but the child's progress is not considered adequate, a statement might be appropriate (7:52–7:67). In paragraph 7:53 the guidance also makes it very clear that the presence of a number of low-level difficulties may not mean that a school cannot make appropriate provision without a statement.

The presence of a statement indicates a high level of input by a range of professionals which must include an Educational Psychologist. Depending on the nature of the child's SEN, others may also have been involved, e.g. specialist support teachers, social workers (education or social services) and/or health workers (e.g. paediatricians, speech and language therapists and physiotherapists). All can offer insights, support and advice. Don't be surprised if this is sometimes conflicting. Remember that each professional will have his/her particular priorities and professional objectives, just as you do. The important thing is that all the professionals concerned liaise as appropriate in order to make sure that the potential for conflicting advice or support is reduced or eliminated.

Gifted, talented and able

Do you know anyone you would consider to be gifted or talented? What do these terms mean to you? Once again we have to contend with a variety of definitions. The DfEE publication *Excellence in Cities* (1999) suggests that the 'very able' are the top 5–10 per cent of the school population. It also refers to gifted and also talented pupils but without defining these terms any further. Belle Wallace (2000) uses the term 'very able' to refer to children who 'need more depth and breadth of work than a teacher normally prepares for a class'. She also brings together a variety of suggestions as to what constitutes giftedness. A number of these refer to the need for a variety of factors to come together in order for giftedness to be present, e.g.:

- above-average ability plus;

- creativity plus; and

- task commitment.

Environmental factors, such as those present in the home and school, like opportunity and stimulation, will also play a significant part. A child may therefore be very able across much of the curriculum or have particular gifts or talents in a specific area such as music, sport or mathematics.

English as an Additional Language (EAL)

As indicated in previous chapters, the Code makes it clear that the fact that English may not be a child's first language does not in itself signify that the child has SEN. It is, however, possible for a child to have EAL *and* to have SEN, so an accurate identification of the child's needs is crucial. Most children pick up a new language with surprising speed but there are a number of strategies that can help in the acquisition of not only an unfamiliar language but also what may be a new culture and different expectations.

Case studies

Throughout this book there are a number of case studies including 'Robert' and 'Jo' below. The purpose of these is made clear in relation to each chapter but they also serve the general purpose of awareness-raising. Case studies in other chapters include 'Jeremy' and 'Sheila' in Chapter 6 and 'Chris' and 'Suki' in Chapter 7. They are only 'snapshots' but I hope they will help you to appreciate the individual nature of each and every learner.

ROBERT

Robert was 5 and had been at school for two terms. His mother was highly relieved that Robert, an only child, had started school as she found him difficult to handle and exhausting to be with. He was 'on the go' all the time, slept very little, so nights were disturbed, and she reported that he didn't concentrate on anything for more than a few seconds. His father worked away from home for much of the time and the rest of the family lived in another part of the country so Robert's mother had little day-to-day support. It was only a matter of a few days after Robert started school before his teacher alerted the SENCO and head teacher to Robert's behaviour and the difficulties she was having in managing him. She also talked to Robert's mother and it soon became clear that Robert's behaviour was a very real cause for concern. The LEA support services were called in and, over a period of several months, Robert was assessed by the Educational Psychologist and a paediatric consultant while the teacher, SENCO and Robert's mother were supported in various ways by a behaviour support teacher, education social worker and social services. Finally, a diagnosis was made. Robert had Attention Deficit Disorder. Robert's mother was greatly relieved as she had blamed herself for his behaviour. The process of statutory assessment was started and Robert's consultant started him on Ritalin treatment. Getting the right dosage proved difficult and affected Robert's behaviour in a number of ways – at one time he was very sleepy and difficult to motivate, then he stabilised and became more responsive but without the same degree of challenging behaviour. After a period of time, however, the effects seemed to wear off and Robert was back to a similar state to that in which he had started school. It was very much a case of one step forward and one step back and, of course, there was no magic solution to his difficulties in the classroom. The class teacher still had to consider what Robert's needs were at any particular time and to try to address these.

JO

Jo is in Year 8 and has a reputation as the class clown. Most of his teachers feel that he is academically more capable than his achievements suggest. Some feel he is making little effort and that his low level disruptive behaviour is the cause of his lack of progress.

Jo's parents are increasingly concerned. While at primary school, Jo seemed to do quite well, although, in hindsight, they realise that he had become an increasingly reluctant reader in Years 5 and 6 and didn't seem to be very interested in writing, although very knowledgeable and articulate. The behaviour problems became more acute when they moved some distance away just before Jo started at secondary school.

Jo's parents were dismayed when they were asked at a recent parents' evening to meet with the SENCO and Jo's head of year because his behaviour in a number of lessons was becoming increasingly disruptive. They are anxiously awaiting the outcome of this meeting.

Figure 3.1　Case studies – Robert and Jo

REFLECTION POINTS

Some suggestions follow for use as starting points for further thought or group discussion.

1. To what extent do you feel that the broad categories of need as provided in the SEN Code of Practice (DfES 2001b) (a) avoid labelling children and (b) provide a useful framework for SEN identification, assessment and provision?

2. How far, in your experience, does the SEN Code of Practice reflect or challenge the public's view of special educational needs and disability?

3. There is an old saying that 'a little knowledge is a dangerous thing'. How, if at all, do you think this might relate to you as a trainee, newly qualified teacher or teaching assistant when working with a class which includes a child who has a physical difficulty about which you know little or nothing?

4. Do you know anyone you would consider to be gifted or talented? What do you think these terms mean? What do they mean to you?

5. What additional strategies might help a child who is unfamiliar with both our language and culture? What would be the first steps you would take (a) before he/she arrived in your school (assuming you had notice) and (b) on his/her arrival in your classroom? Would it make any difference if there were other children in the class who spoke the new child's mother tongue?

Identification, assessment and support

The previous chapter gave a very basic introduction to the range of special educational needs. This chapter considers how these needs might be addressed by teachers or those who support them. It begins by considering the identification and assessment of needs and how you might go about this. It then explores the management of the resources you might have available before moving on to consider a number of the most common areas of difficulty and basic supportive strategies for each. Subsequent chapters, especially 6 and 7, will provide a broader context for managing these strategies within the inclusive classroom.

Induction Standard c

QtT S3.1.1, all of section S3.2

Identification and assessment of needs

Identification

In some cases children will have been identified as having special educational needs before they start school. This is more likely to be the case if the difficulties are severe and/or physically obvious, e.g. Down's syndrome or a physical disability. Sometimes a difficulty or disability will be obvious at, or soon after, birth but in other cases it, or the extent of its impact, will only be apparent at a later stage. Some needs may only become evident after a child has started school, e.g. those associated with reading or writing. In other cases a child may not have special educational needs at all but teaching and learning strategies, inappropriate expectations or the curriculum itself may be the cause of the difficulties. As you will probably have realised, the diagnosis of a difficulty may be far from simple, although parents will often, understandably, want to know the reason for their child's difficulties and place a high priority on establishing this. Clearly, discovering the cause of the difficulty will, in many cases, assist the teacher in planning appropriate strategies to support the child's learning, but if you wait for this you may lose valuable learning time. Identifying the child's *needs* will enable the teacher to plan as effectively as possible. As further information becomes available, and the child, hopefully, progresses, planning will need to reflect this.

The elimination of some potential causes of difficulty can sometimes be relatively straightforward, e.g. a visual difficulty or problems at home. It is always useful to remove potential causes from your list of possibilities so that you can focus on the most appropriate lines of enquiry and strategies for teaching and learning. You should also bear in mind that it is often a group of difficulties rather than an individual problem that will suggest a particular diagnosis.

Data can be collected from a variety of sources, both informal and formal, e.g.:

- Baseline or other screening, standardised tests etc. Some of these may have taken place before the child enters school; others will have taken place subsequently. Do treat standardised test results with caution and remember that different tests set out to analyse or investigate different elements of a skill such as reading.

- School records. These may indicate what has been of concern in the past, action taken and the results of this, the child's strengths, achievements etc.

- Classroom observation by teacher – what the child can do, finds difficult or does differently, together with the context in which this happens.

- Information from the parents/carers.

- Information from the child – dialogue, games/activities etc.

- Information from previous teachers, SENCO or other professionals.

- Evaluation of the child's learning.

- Results of trying different strategies, e.g. changing the child's working environment, by sitting at a different table or in a different position, using more ICT etc.

Circumstances will vary. Sometimes you may have very little to go on if, for example, a child has just arrived from abroad and the family speak little or no English, or if a child is just starting school or moving to a new area before any records have arrived or any testing has taken place. At other times you may be almost overwhelmed with the amount of information you are given, especially if it is conflicting or presented in a way that is not easy to access. To be really helpful the data you collect should:

- provide objective information about what a child can or cannot do and the context in which any achievement takes place;

- provide an indication of a child's strengths as well as weaknesses, including test results, National Curriculum levels etc.;

- indicate what the child is interested in or enjoys, i.e. things the child finds rewarding or pleasurable; and

- include any strategies that have been found to be helpful or unhelpful in supporting the child's learning.

Assessment

This is the further analysis of the nature of the child's or young person's needs so that appropriate provision can be made in the classroom. Appropriate provision will include the setting of achievable targets and a plan of action. Through assessment you will be aiming to identify:

- which needs are the priorities;

- targets to meet these needs; and

- the information you will require to produce an appropriate action plan, e.g. resources that might be appropriate to meet these needs.

Induction Standard c

QtT S3.1.1, all of section S3.2

HLTA all of section 3.2

Sometimes a child will have a significant number of needs which cannot all be addressed at once. Some will be of greater priority than others in any period. Assessment should help you to decide on priorities.

There are two broad types of assessment: summative and formative. If you are looking at someone else's assessment you need to know what type of assessment it is in order to be able to make appropriate use of the information it is providing. Similarly, if you are carrying out an assessment you need to know what it is that you are trying to find out and therefore what type of assessment will best meet those needs.

The majority of primary and secondary aged pupils with SEN will be assessed with their peers at National Curriculum levels. However, for those unlikely to reach beyond level 2 by the time they leave secondary school, P-levels have been developed as a form of teacher assessment for pupils. Many LAs provide training in the use of P-levels and staff in your local special schools will also have experience of using them.

Classroom observation is a powerful tool and there is a section on this in Chapter 8 in the context of school visits and school experience during Initial Teacher Training (ITT) in particular. This, coupled with any information you can gather from parents and the child, will be extremely useful as you are in a position to decide what areas will be the most beneficial to focus upon. There may, for example, be a need to reduce a child's disruptive behaviour before concentrating on reading or spelling difficulties or to prioritise reading skills before addressing writing. Having some insights into the child's strengths and weaknesses allows you to find suitable starting points so that you can build on the child's previous learning and also build in success and achievement. An awareness of a child's interests can also help you to make a positive start as described in Chapter 7. QtT Standards 3.1.1, 3.1.2, 3.2.1 and 3.2.6 are particularly relevant here.

Table 4.1   Types of assessment

Summative assessment	Formative assessment
Provides a snapshot of what a child can or cannot do at a particular point in time	Ongoing and cyclical, so gives a picture of progress over a period of time
Will confirm if a child is behind or ahead of other children of similar age	Provides feedback and can support planning and learning progression
e.g. a baseline or standardised test	e.g. marking and the records kept of this, diagnostic tests (tests designed to pinpoint areas of strength or difficulty)

Resources and their management

There are two main forms of resource that a teacher has access to:

1. human resources – those of the child, yourself and other people (both adults and children); and

2. material resources.

Your resources

Your attitude to diversity and differences will play a significant part in the meeting of a child's needs. If there is effective planning with achievable targets and high expectations, it gives a powerful signal to the child or young person that he/she can achieve and be successful. It does not matter how experienced or otherwise you may be; if you have a less than positive attitude towards those with special educational needs the signal to your class will be obvious.

The resources of the child

Every child will have strengths as well as weaknesses/difficulties, preferred learning style and interests. Identifying and making use of these will go a considerable way towards providing the optimum learning experience for the child.

The resources of other children

If each child has strengths, weaknesses and interests, it follows that groups of children can be formed that will complement each other for a particular task or activity. Static groupings can be very limiting and, if organised by ability or achievement, are soon recognised as such by the children. It does not take long for the self-esteem of a child perceived to be always in the 'bottom' or 'special needs' group to be dented. Groupings are explored further in Chapter 6.

The resources of other adults

These may include:

- teachers, including the SENCO;
- support/teaching assistants;
- lunchtime supervisors;
- other adult volunteers;
- those on work experience placements;
- trainee teachers;
- professionals from outside agencies including the LEA, e.g. specialist support teachers, Educational Psychologists (EPs), education social workers, and colleagues from health and social services etc.

QtT S3.1.4 refers to planning for other adults in the classroom as appropriate

Induction Standards a and e

HLTA 3.1.1, 3.2.1

Classrooms will have the resources of other adults available in them and, as a teacher, this will give you tremendous help if (but only if) these resources are used effectively. This requires careful planning and liaison. Always bear in mind that other colleagues in the classroom will always do what they think is best in the absence of any direction or discussion. This may not be what you had in mind or expected and can then lead you, potentially, into making incorrect judgements about the child's ability and achievement if you are not aware of what has been done and how.

Material resources

Material resources cover a huge range including:

- aids and equipment, e.g. low vision aids such as magnifiers, sloping desk supports, pencil grips;
- ICT hardware, e.g. computers and accessories to enable computer access, photocopiers, digital cameras, video/DVD, personal radio/CD player, audio recording equipment, interactive whiteboards;
- ICT software to address specific needs, e.g. Write from the Start, Wordshark, Numbershark (see Resources and further reading, p. 102);
- courses/schemes of work; and
- photocopiable and pre-prepared resources, e.g. recording sheets, worksheets, number squares etc.

Knowing what is available to you in the school or department in which you are working and what is available from your provider, if you are a trainee, is important. Bear in mind that the attitude of schools towards making resources available during school experience is highly variable and also that it is unrealistic to expect to know *all* that is available in the school in the short time you may have. This is particularly so for ICT software because you need to do more than just quickly scan programs in order to be able to use them effectively in the classroom. Using the programs can be time-consuming. However, please do not let this put you off taking every possible opportunity to explore the potential of different programs. Make a note of anything that might be useful to you in the future.

Reading, spelling and writing

These three activities are inextricably bound together and difficulties in one area will usually have some impact on the others. All three are very complex activities which require the coming together of a range of skills. The identification and assessment of a child's particular needs are therefore crucial if appropriate teaching and learning strategies are to be initiated. Put in very simple terms, there are two major elements in the act of reading:

1. Making the connection between the symbols and the word they represent (decoding); and
2. Understanding the words that have been decoded.

Don't be misled into thinking that because a child can decode well, and therefore appears to read fluently, he/she can necessarily understand or comprehend the text. Both decoding and comprehension are needed for reading.

The pre-reading stage

There are a number of indications at a pre-reading stage that a child *may* have difficulties with reading. These include:

- difficulty in discriminating between sounds;
- poor sequencing skills;
- difficulty with matching pictures or shapes;

- poor oral language or a history of language delay;
- poor hand–eye or motor control; and
- poor auditory and/or visual memory, e.g. difficulty with remembering nursery rhymes.

It is well worth keeping a watchful eye and ensuring that opportunities are provided for children to develop these skills. However, it is also quite difficult to determine whether a perceived difficulty is a developmental delay that will correct itself or whether it really is a cause for concern. The teacher needs to keep a careful note of progress.

Early reading

At this stage the child will not have built up a sufficiently large sight vocabulary to be able to read text without needing to decode unfamiliar words. It therefore follows that the child needs to have an approach for decoding. Phonic teaching works well for many children and is currently frequently promoted as a key element in learning to read, write and spell. However, some children do find it hard to work with parts of words and to build them up into a whole, because they tend to work the opposite way round, i.e. from whole to part. A structured, phonic approach will help many but learning to decode by breaking words up into sounds, as phonic readers do, will not work for all children. Taking a multi-sensory approach (see Chapter 7) to visualising whole words, as well as working on phonics, may be a more successful strategy and equally useful for the older child or adult who has failed to learn to read.

Later reading (primary stage)

By this stage a child should have built up a reasonable sight vocabulary thus no longer needing to decode every word. If a child has only a small sight vocabulary, fluency and understanding of reading material will become increasingly problematic. Reading will be a slow process and thus will impact increasingly on many areas of the curriculum.

Later reading (secondary stage)

Difficulties will become increasingly obvious as a young person moves into secondary schooling. In many areas of the secondary curriculum there is a high dependence on the reading and writing ability of the learner. Sight-recognition and learning the meaning and spelling of key specialist words will become increasingly important if academic progress is to be seen to be made and written evidence provided by the learner. A more able young person with some dyslexic tendencies may have successfully masked his/her reading difficulties at primary school only to find this increasingly hard at secondary school.

Readability

For independent reading, a child should be able to read 95 per cent of the words in the text and for instructional reading at least 90 per cent. As the percentage of words a child or young person can read decreases, frustration level may be reached, which is clearly not desirable. For any of the support strategies that follow, the level of readability must be right.

Ways of helping children to minimise their error level when, for example, taking part in guided reading might include:

- the introduction of new vocabulary by talking through each page before the guided reading begins; and

- revising key initial sounds or word endings that are relevant to the book/passage.

Careful introduction of subject-specific or specialised vocabulary is equally important at the secondary stage.

Pause, prompt and praise

This is a useful technique for supporting a child with reading. Although the term 'teacher' has been used in the outline below, this could be any helper who has been taken through what is required of him/her. It is, of course, important to make sure the readability level is right so that the child does not reach frustration level. The steps are as follows:

1. The child reads the passage to the teacher.
2. The child stops when he/she reaches an unknown word.
3. The teacher pauses to allow the child a short time to work out what the word is.
4. If the child is unable to work out what the word is, the teacher prompts the child, e.g. 'Can you guess what the word might be; look at the initial letter; what sound does it make?' etc.
5. If the child produces the correct word the teacher praises him/her.
6. If the child does not produce the correct word after the brief prompt, the teacher supplies the word.

The teacher also praises for self-correcting.

Comprehension

Reading can only be said to be taking place if the child can understand what he/she is reading as well as being able to decode. Ways of supporting a child in developing greater comprehension skills could include:

- previewing a passage before reading;
- predicting what might happen next;
- retelling the story or summarising part of the passage;
- encouraging children to ask each other relevant questions; and
- use of strategies such as cloze procedure (see below).

Many of these strategies are equally useful at both primary and secondary levels.

Cloze procedure

Take the text and remove every fifth or sixth word. The child then has to provide the missing words. This can help a child to use context cues. Variations on the theme could include missing out the initial letter of some words or even several consecutive words.

There is also a wide range of software available to support a learner with reading and spelling difficulties, e.g. Wordshark (published by White Space), which has games suitable for KS1 to KS3.

Spelling

Spelling requires a set of skills which involves eyes, ears and hands.

- Eyes – we often know when a word 'looks right' and, as previously mentioned, some children do see the whole word rather than the parts of a word.

- Ears – the child needs to be able to discriminate between sounds and to blend sounds.

- Hands – the memory and feeling of hand movements needed for writing particular sounds or combinations of sounds and whole words. Once there is a flow and the child stops thinking letter by letter, spelling tends to improve. This is the reason why some teachers advocate learning cursive writing from the start as it can aid writing flow.

Difficulties with spelling will hinder progress in a number of ways, e.g.:

- the flow of thought can be interrupted when writing as a child or young person stops to work on a spelling;

- it can hamper comprehension when reading;

- more time may be spent on spelling rather than content; and

- the whole process of reading or writing can be dramatically lengthened.

You will need to ascertain what the particular difficulties are and the following categories of error may help you with this:

- Random or bizarre – no obvious spelling strategy is used and the reader finds it very difficult to read the word at all.

- Invented or unreasonable – the reader makes an attempt to use visual and/or phonetic strategies but is still dependent on the sound–symbol relationship, e.g. shod (showed).

- Plausible or reasonable – the reader uses patterns found in English spelling, e.g. brooze (bruise), sum (some).

The link between spelling and handwriting is of great importance and Chapters 6 and 7 provide some further information, particularly in the section on multi-sensory teaching and learning. Some of the strategies outlined below make use of this link.

Look, cover, write and check

- LOOK at the word. Note any parts you can spell. What is the difficult bit? Underlining this part or going over it with colour may help.

- COVER the word.

- WRITE the word. Say the letters as you go and use cursive/joined-up writing where possible.

- CHECK the word is correctly spelt.

Look, remember, cover, write, check and say

This is a variation of Look, cover, write and check with a couple of extra steps which make fuller use of the different senses. Remembering is the positive act of committing the spelling or part of it to memory. This might include the use of colour, visualising the word in the mind's eye or other strategies that will aid recall. The final step is the saying out loud of the letter names and/or sounds in order, which, again, will help to aid memory and recall.

Other strategies might include:

- teaching spelling rules;

- repeated writing;

- games, activities and puzzles for overlearning;

- making word chains – take the root of a word and then add to it, e.g. jump, jumping etc.;

- developing a personal word bank for a learner; and

- developing recall strategies, e.g. use of mnemonics.

Writing

There are a number of factors which might impact on a child's writing abilities, e.g.:

- reading and/or spelling difficulties;

- language delay or disorder;

- poor fine motor control; and

- poor sequencing or organisational skills.

Some useful strategies might include:

- the use of flow charts or mind maps (see Chapter 7);

- brainstorming before writing – discussion, making connections, e.g. take a key word and mind map connections, e.g. *castle* – fights, war, thick walls, moat, knights, arrow slits, cold, dungeons; or *production* – factories, lines, growing, making;

- providing a sentence or part sentence as a starting point;

- prompts, e.g. 'What happened next? What did X do? What did it look like?' etc.;

- work on joining words so that sentences are combined or on descriptive words so that vocabulary is increased;

- making a book;

- writing a script for an interview or television show;

- use of computer prediction programs such as Penfriend (Inclusive), Prophet (ACE Centre) or TextHelp (Analyst);

- working on just part of the writing process, e.g. planning, drafting or editing. This could be presented as taking a different role, e.g. editor or author;

- use of a writing frame or template with headings;

- use of word processing facilities to 'cut and paste'.

Handwriting

The causes of poor handwriting are many and may include one or more of the following:

- poor hand–eye co-ordination as a result, for example, of dyspraxia;

- poor fine motor control;

- uncomfortable or inappropriate pencil grip;

- inappropriate position for writing;

- if left-handed, sitting close and to the right of another child who is right-handed (or vice versa);

- establishment of incorrect letter formation which then interferes with the flow of writing;

- having to think about spelling, text organisation etc. to such an extent that it interferes with handwriting fluency (e.g. dyslexia);

- visual difficulties that make it difficult for the child to see or copy text or to follow a demonstration;

- inadequate time on pre-writing skills of pattern formation, pencil control etc.;

- use of writing materials that do not match the child's ability.

Identification of the difficulty will help you to choose an appropriate strategy so the following check may help:

1. Is the writing instrument held correctly and comfortably? Pencil grips can be useful for all ages and will encourage an appropriate pencil hold. There are a variety of grips available from a simple triangular one to more sophisticated grips which encourage the fingertips to remain in the correct position (stockists include LDA). These can be useful for all ages and are an inexpensive resource. Chubby pencils are also available.

2. Is the child sitting in an appropriate position and with the paper in an appropriate position too? Remember that the left-handed position is different from the right-handed one, and make sure the child is sitting on the appropriate side of others for his/her respective handedness. Desk slopes and/or aids for securing paper can be very useful. Commercial aids are available and in many

cases worth purchasing for longer-term use. However, there are various things you can do to try out the possible effectiveness of such aids. A drawing-board or clipboard can be supported by a book to form a slope and Blu-tack®, masking tape or the clip can secure the paper.

3. Is there difficulty with controlling the pencil or pen? If so, does the child have fine motor control difficulties when engaged in other activities?

Many young children need plenty of practice with pre-writing pattern-making and there are a number of commercially produced worksheets for this.

Table 4.2   Poor organisational skills

Problem	Possible cause	Possible solution(s)
Letters or notes not getting home	Poor memory: child forgets to deliver	Teacher and parent work together, e.g. teacher puts any messages in the home-to-school including the fact that the child has a letter. Parent asks child each evening if he/she has any notes from school and checks the school bag.
Young person doesn't hand in homework	Difficulties with copying from whiteboard and writing down homework task quickly enough at the end of lessons.	Teacher discusses possible solutions with youngster, e.g. allowing more time for writing down homework at the end of the lesson, putting details up at an earlier stage in the lesson, providing a printout of homework tasks.
Child takes longer than others to undress for PE	Poor fine motor control so child has difficulty with buttons and shoelaces	Teacher and parent work together, e.g. consider together what type of fastenings the child might find easier to cope with so that this can be taken into account next time clothes are purchased, e.g. Velcro fasteners instead of shoelaces, fewer and/or larger buttons, buttons on elastic. Teach child how to tie shoelaces and provide practice time. Provide more time for child to undress, e.g. perhaps starting earlier than other children. Set up a time challenge for the child to see if he/she can beat his/her best time for undressing.
	Sequencing difficulties so unsure which clothing item to attend to in which order	Doll with paper clothes with tabs on. With support of teaching assistant, child practises dressing and undressing the doll. When this is learnt, TA undresses doll at same time as child undresses until child able to undress without the doll.

Organisational skills

Clearly, organisational expectations will depend upon a number of things, e.g. the age of the child, temperament and motivation as well as specific skills, abilities and experiences such as:

- memory
- sequencing
- concept of time
- sense of direction
- learning style preferences
- speed of writing or reading

Number manipulation and mathematical skills

In the previous chapter we considered a range of needs and how they manifested themselves. The following examples show how these might impact on a child's or young person's learning in the areas of numeracy and mathematics:

- Short-term memory – difficulty with remembering a sequence of instructions for computation or for drawing an accurate diagram.
- Long-term memory – difficulty with remembering routines, linking mathematical topics, recalling tables or formulae.
- Directional confusion – knowing the correct place to start with a computation (e.g. a vertical tens and units addition would usually be started from the right with the units but we read from left to right), remembering which is left and right, working round a decimal point, use of rotation, using a number line.
- Visual perception – identification of similar looking symbols, e.g. 3, 5 and 2; 6 and 9; + and ×.
- Sequencing problems – counting forwards or backwards, recalling days of the week, recalling tables.
- Spatial awareness – place value, copying from the board, nominators and denominators, making links between two- and three-dimensional representations.
- Language – verbal sums, reading a maths question, naming symbols, double-meaning words, e.g. right and write, units (kitchen units or tens and units).
- Problem solving – difficulty with reading/understanding written problems – the youngster may not be a logical thinker or may have difficulty in making the links between symbols and reality.
- Motor difficulties – difficulty with cutting out shapes, holding a ruler steady, drawing diagrams.

Careful planning will be of considerable help. Think about your intended outcomes and how best these can be achieved by the child. Is cutting out the shapes going to help the child distinguish between a triangle and square, for example, or can you, for a child with motor difficulties, find another learning activity which will serve the same purpose? This is not to suggest that there is no place for providing a child with learning opportunities and practice in order to enhance cutting skills, but this might be more appropriately provided at another time. Basic strategies and ideas for material resources that may prove useful include the following, but this is by no means an exhaustive list:

- Concrete aids before abstract ideas. This is a good phrase to remember. Provide opportunities for the use of concrete aids and use them during your demonstrations.

- Introduce new vocabulary right from the beginning of the topic and use it consistently. Find different ways of reinforcing this, e.g. by use of questions, discussion, checking understanding, asking the child to tell and show, i.e. use concrete aids to demonstrate what he/she is going to do while telling you in a step-by-step way using the appropriate language.

- Revisit topics regularly and make links with other topics and concepts that have already been introduced, e.g. multiplication as repeated addition.

- Number lines, number squares, number fans – on tables, walls as appropriate.

- Audio tapes of tables or formulae that must be remembered and recalled easily.

- Concrete aids such as Unifix cubes, plastic money, counters, clock faces with synchronised hands, timers.

- Task sheets that have instructional symbols or pictures to reduce the level of reading required.

- Software such as Numbershark (published by White Space).

Westwood (1997) gives a good basic assessment checklist for different stages but the following questions may help you to gather some useful assessment information to aid your planning:

- Can he/she do this with concrete aids?

- Can he/she explain what has to be done?

- Can he/she show me step by step?

- What can he/she do with and without guidance or prompts?

- Does he/she understand the key terms and concepts involved?

Social skills

Social skills are the verbal and non-verbal competencies of initiating and maintaining contact with others, e.g. taking turns, maintaining eye contact when speaking or listening to others, controlling anger, awareness of personal space, appropriate use of voice and gesture. If, for whatever reason, a child lacks some of the social skills that are appropriate for his/her age, the child will have difficulty in behaving in a way which supports classroom learning. The child's behaviour may, especially if it is overt, also impact upon your teaching.

There may be a number of reasons for a child having social difficulties, e.g.:

- family circumstances;
- lack of opportunity to socialise at a pre-school stage;
- a learning difficulty that has resulted in low self-esteem; or
- a specific disorder, e.g. ADHD.

Observation will play a critical part in identifying and assessing needs and the following questions provide a good starting point:

- What does the child/young person do, and in what circumstances?
- What doesn't the child/young person do, and in what circumstances?
- What are the priorities to work on, bearing in mind what would be appropriate for the context in which the child/young person is learning and what would make the greatest positive impact?

Social skills can be taught. Circle time can be an excellent strategy (see Chapter 7) but some may need specific teaching on an individual basis. The following model may be useful in that situation:

Model, rehearse, feedback, use and reinforce

- Model – the adult models the required behaviour.
- Imitate/rehearse – the child imitates and rehearses the behaviour.
- The adult provides feedback and reinforcement.
- Opportunities are provided to reinforce the skill.
- Reinforcement is provided, e.g. praise, reward.

Strategies such as addressing social issues as part of class topics or PSHE can be useful too, e.g. making friends, keeping safe, making presentations, managing anger. Throughout this chapter we have looked at strategies for identifying and assessing needs and also at some basic approaches that you might try. Remember

Imran invades the personal space of others when standing and talking to them. He tends to go right up to both adults and other children and to stand about thirty centimetres away from them. As a result the person usually steps back but Imran then moves forward. Other children are now avoiding Imran in the playground because of their discomfort.

Both Imran's teacher and teaching assistant modelled the required behaviour. They showed Imran the distance between them when they talked and then demonstrated this by approaching Imran so that he understood and could see and feel the appropriate distance between them. He then practised approaching the two adults at specific points during the day which had been set aside for this. The adults gave him praise and feedback as appropriate. When Imran was able to judge the distance without prompts he was given opportunities to practise by, for example, being sent to deliver messages to other adults in the school or to groups of children during PE lessons.

Figure 4.1 Case study – Imran (Year 4)

that there are plenty of people who can provide support and information to help you. You can play your part by ensuring that the information you give them in the first place enables them to support you appropriately. Gathering objective and relevant information along the lines suggested will make their task that much easier. If, on the other hand, you approach the SENCO, for example, and say that Rob is being difficult, the SENCO will have a great deal of probing to do before being able to make suggestions as to how you might proceed.

The same principles of gathering information in order to identify and assess needs and then planning to meet them applies to your work with all children including the gifted and talented and those for whom English is an additional language. Try to get some groundwork done first. It need not take a large amount of time but if you set about gathering information in a systematic and considered way it will pay dividends in terms of the learning that takes place in your classroom.

Induction
Standard c

QtT S3.2.5

QtT S3.1.3

HLTA
3.1.3,
3.2.2

REFLECTION POINTS

The following suggestions may help you to gather evidence of meeting standards and/or provide starting points for further discussion:

1. In this chapter we have concentrated on the needs of children with a range of learning difficulties. What sort of information and data would be useful for you to collect in order to identify the needs of a child who is gifted and talented or for whom English is an additional language?

2. Make a note of any reading schemes or resource series you come across and how children with different needs respond to the different series.

CHAPTER 5

Inclusion and related issues

In this chapter we will think about issues of equality, inclusion and exclusion. Our starting point will be to consider the legislation and documentation that provides us with the broad framework in which we work. We will then consider the impact this has on us as teachers. Suggestions will also be made for further reading and exploration.

Standards S3.3.14 (QtT) and 3.3.7 (HLTA) challenge you to 'recognise and respond effectively to equal opportunities issues as they arise in the classroom'. The standards go on to provide examples of when you should be able to do this, including challenging bullying and harassment, and stereotypical views. It is impossible for these standards to be met unless you consider your own attitudes and values. These will be critical in shaping the sort of teacher or teaching assistant you become. They are fundamental to your approach to working with children with a wide range of needs and backgrounds. Please take time to explore this thoroughly and to think about some of the questions posed in this chapter.

Legislation and documentation

Equality

The United Kingdom supports the Salamanca Statement (UNESCO 1994), which was drawn up by a United Nations Educational, Scientific and Cultural Organization (UNESCO) conference in 1994. The statement calls upon all governments to subscribe to the principle of inclusive education for all children in regular (mainstream) schools wherever possible.

Integration and inclusion

Integration

We briefly looked at integration in Chapter 1 when considering the Warnock Report (DES 1978). You may remember that the report recommended that there should be a range of provision to include mainstream with support, special schools, units attached to mainstream schools and, where appropriate, education at home. Integration featured strongly with three levels being identified: locational, social and functional. There is, at least to some extent, an implication that integration is 'bolted on' to existing mainstream provision. The term 'integration' was officially used from the publication of the Warnock Report until 1997.

Inclusion

The term 'inclusion', on the other hand, implies that *including* all children is the starting point rather than adding children with special needs to a system and situation which already exists. It is a process which requires the development of policies, cultures and practices and the removal of barriers to learning and participation. It involves rights and entitlements. Inclusion is about more than classroom practice or, indeed, education. It is a far-reaching and challenging concept which relates to all areas of our lives and society at large.

Excellence for All Children: Meeting Special Educational Needs was published by the DfEE in 1997 and this highlighted the fact that inclusion was now part of official central government policy. *Inclusive Schooling* (DfES 2001a) is the statutory guidance on the operation of the government's inclusion framework (sections 316, 316A and schedule 27 in the 1996 Education Act).

Exclusion

The law relating to exclusions from school is set out in the Education Act 2002. The most recent regulations, which came into force on 20 January 2003, are to be found in The Education (Pupils' Exclusions and Appeals) (Maintained Schools) (England) Regulations 2002 (S.1.2002/3178) and in The Education (Pupils' Exclusions and Appeals) (Pupil Referral Units) (England) Regulations 2002 (S.1.2002/3179).

A head teacher in England can formally exclude a pupil for up to 45 days in any one school year (fixed-term exclusion) or permanently. In the case of a fixed-term exclusion, the length of the exclusion has to be stated at the outset. A pupil can also be excluded from the school premises for lunchtimes for a fixed period. Each lunchtime counts as half a day.

Every governing body and LEA has procedures in place for dealing with formal exclusions. The DfES has produced guidance relating to exclusions and details about this can be found at the end of this chapter. Guidance relating to the exclusion of pupils with SEN is to be found in the SEN Code of Practice.

Inclusion and exclusion in practice

As we delve more deeply into the meaning of inclusion and inclusive practice, I would like to invite you to think about Carpenter and Ashdown's (2001) suggestions as to the nature of inclusion and then to consider the four key principles of inclusion published by NASEN (2002).

Carpenter and Ashdown (2001) suggest that:

Inclusion:

● Is premised on diversity

● Is multidimensional

● Applies to individuals

● Applies to all learners

● Is diagnostic

● Challenges expectations

● Challenges classroom relationships

- Is an integral aspect of effective learning
- Is relevant to all teachers
- Requires a long-term, whole-school strategy

NASEN has published a policy statement on inclusion in which it states four key principles:

- Every human being has an entitlement to personal, social and intellectual development and must be given an opportunity to achieve his/her potential in learning.
- Every human being is unique in terms of characteristics, interests, abilities, motivation and learning needs.
- Educational systems should be designed to take into account these wide diversities.
- Those with exceptional learning needs and/or disabilities should have access to high quality and appropriate education.

Figure 5.1 NASEN (2002) policy document on inclusion

Read through these again and think about your initial responses.

Diversity is a key word in both and is viewed positively. For inclusion to take place, diversity needs to be acknowledged as both existing and as being a positive asset in the classroom. Where this is not the case, a school culture is unlikely to embrace inclusion fully as part of its organisational culture. If diversity is acknowledged and seen in a positive light, inclusion becomes both possible and inseparable from effective teaching and learning.

You can't just 'do' inclusion or equality on one level, e.g. making sure all children have a turn at being at the front of the line; it has to be something that permeates every aspect of the school, its organisation and culture. If inclusion applies to every single individual in the school, there can be no exceptions. Inclusion cannot be something that is 'done' only to children with SEN. It applies to everyone equally. It therefore follows that it must be relevant to everyone in the school including all adults who work in the school. No-one can be absolved from the responsibility to ensure that inclusion is a reality for everyone in the school. That inclusion challenges thinking, expectations and values is therefore clear.

If all this is accepted, it is clear that practice does not and will not change overnight. A long-term strategy is needed for inclusion to become embedded and practised. A school will need to question what the barriers are to learning and participation and what can be done to minimise or remove them.

The NASEN policy statement begins with notions of entitlement and opportunity for all. A positive view of diversity underpins the policy together with an acknowledgement of the breadth of diversity that must be taken into account by educational systems. This is a huge challenge especially when the extreme ends of the continuum of need are taken into account as well, hence the final bullet point. The needs of some learners will be easier to take into account than others and attitudes to the needs of some will be more positive than others.

Consider the list below and then rank it in order of ease of including a child with these needs or difficulties in a mainstream classroom. You may want to consider this in the context of a particular key stage or age range. Of necessity, these are very brief 'pen pictures', but I hope that they provide you with some food for thought and perhaps be the basis for discussion with other trainees and teachers you meet during your training. While you are completing this, think about stereotyping and if that is a trap you fall into sometimes.

> **A** Child/young person has a severe visual impairment and sees only some light and dark. Uses Braille and a Braille machine. Full-time support assistant. Bright and outgoing.
>
> **B** Refugee child or young person recently arrived. English not spoken or understood by family on arrival. No-one in the school community speaks their home language.
>
> **C** Child or young person with dyslexia. Spatial awareness is exceptionally good and excels in many sports and also in art (drawing and sculpture being particular interests). Oral skills good but reading and writing very poor.
>
> **D** Child or young person with behavioural and social difficulties. In the care of third set of foster parents. Unsettled and hits out at other children when angry or frustrated. Has missed a lot of schooling so has many gaps but does enjoy, and is very good at, PE.

Figure 5.2 Pen pictures

When I have done a similar exercise with trainees a number of issues generally form a focus for discussion and you might like to compare your thoughts with some of the following points raised by other trainees and teachers:

- concern about doing the right thing and lack of confidence in dealing with a particular set of needs which a mainstream teacher or teaching assistant may see as requiring specialised knowledge and skill;
- the attitude of the senior management, the teachers and teaching assistants, the parents/carers and the child to the difficulties or needs, and how positive (or otherwise) this is;
- concern about the level of disruption in the classroom and the impact this will have on the learning and/or behaviour of others in the classroom;
- levels of empathy and sympathy for different needs; there is often more sympathy for pupil A, for example, than there is for D;
- the extent to which it is felt that the child or young person has control over his/her difficulties. Again, D is sometimes seen as potentially having more control than the other children;
- the nature of the difficulty in terms of how long term or otherwise it might be. B, for example, may be expected to overcome his/her difficulties in a relatively short time as he/she acquires a working knowledge of the language. A, on the other hand, may have a permanent visual impairment;
- the level of adult support in the classroom is often seen as a crucial factor in terms of the teacher's ability to cope with this level of need in a mainstream classroom. Other factors suggested are the experience of the teacher and the levels of support from teaching assistants, parents, the LEA support services and senior management.

differences of treatment and those which go against the whole idea of inclusion and equality? The following mini case studies are designed to provide examples of the tensions a class teacher might experience and some of the questions raised.

CASE STUDY 1

Class 2F is a mixed-ability class of six- and seven-year-old children. The class has access to the school's ICT suite once a week and the range of achievement across the class is widening as the school year goes on. Some of the children have access to computers at home and are very confident in using them. Others only ever use a computer at school and are still struggling with finding their way round the keyboard and using a mouse.

The class teacher feels that there is a real tension between maintaining the motivation and achievement of the children who are confident and supporting the others so as to enhance and build upon their limited experience. The teacher feels that there is an inevitability about the widening gap between these two groups as the confident children have, generally speaking, the advantages of home support and much greater access to computers and other new technologies. In many, but not all, cases, the children who are achieving less are those who have no access to computers at home and who have additional difficulties such as SEN or poor command of English.

This case study highlights a common dilemma for teachers. How do you balance the needs of children who are already, in some sense, advantaged but who have greater potential in terms of achievement, with the needs of children who are disadvantaged and who may not achieve to the same level as the first group? Use this as a discussion topic and think about both your own values and attitudes as well as practical solutions for this particular teacher.

CASE STUDY 2

Year 6 is split into two classes. The classes are set according to ability for literacy and numeracy every morning. One class teacher takes the lower ability group for literacy and the other for numeracy. Recently there have been discussions between the two teachers and senior management about the advisability or otherwise of setting the children for Science and ICT. Science takes place on one afternoon each week but ICT is on a different afternoon and is timetabled against the use of the hall for PE. Thus one class has ICT followed by PE and the other has PE followed by ICT. The consequence of setting for ICT would be setting for PE as well.

What are the arguments for and against setting 1. in general for children in Year 6 and 2. for each of the subject areas highlighted in this case study (i.e. literacy, numeracy, science, ICT and PE)? Use the concepts of inclusion, exclusion, equality of opportunity and entitlement to support your arguments.

CASE STUDY 3

A senior management team of a large comprehensive school has decided to look again at the issue of setting pupils. A group of teachers have asked that the issue be debated as they feel very strongly that pupils with SEN and other needs, such as those arising from EAL, should not be placed in bottom sets with pupils who are disruptive. Other teachers feel equally strongly that the current setting allows pupils who are more able, who have potential and who want to work to achieve the best possible results, rather than being disadvantaged by having disruptive pupils in their sets.

What is your response to the two sides of this argument?

Figure 5.3   Case studies

The aim of this chapter has been to raise your awareness of issues and to challenge you to think about your own values and attitudes. The suggestions in the Resources and further reading section will provide starting points for further research and reading. There are also some more questions for readers to consider in the Reflection points at the end of this chapter.

The next chapter looks at issues of teaching and learning while Chapter 7 considers teaching approaches. You may like to read these before returning to some of the issues raised in this chapter and considering how these approaches might support inclusive practice in the classroom.

REFLECTION POINTS

The following suggestions may help you to gather evidence of meeting standards and/or provide starting points for further discussion:

1. What would you feel are the main issues for (a) school managers and (b) class/subject teachers in providing an inclusive education for all children?

2. Thomas and Loxley (2001) suggest that 'inclusive education is really about extending the comprehensive ideal of education. Those who talk about it are therefore less concerned with children's supposed "special educational needs" and more concerned with developing an education system in which tolerance, diversity and equity are striven for'. Do you think they are right? What evidence do you see of this being the case?

3. A significant number of pupils excluded from school have special educational needs. Who benefits from such exclusions, and how? What, if any, negative impacts might an exclusion have, and upon whom? What alternatives might there be to this type of exclusion?

4. Think about a school you have recently been in (e.g. as a pupil, trainee or volunteer). What aspects of the school organisation and culture would you view as being inclusive? If you can, consider two or three of the pupils and how barriers to their learning have been or could be minimised.

5. Keep a note of any inclusive practice you see/hear about and how these have removed potential barriers to learning. Where appropriate, adapt these to your own situation.

QtT
S3.3.14

HLTA 3.3.7

QtT
S3.3.4,
S3.3.6

HLTA 3.3.5

PART 2

Theory into Practice

Teaching and learning

This chapter seeks to challenge your thinking about teaching and learning in general as well as in relation to special educational needs. It suggests paths to explore and issues to consider by taking a number of ideas and theories and exploring how these may influence the way in which we set about teaching our classes. There are a number of excellent texts, some of which are referred to in this book, which are devoted to teaching and learning theory and which explore many more issues and in far greater depth. The main aim of this chapter is to encourage you to think about a particularly difficult and emotive question: 'Do all children who are failing at school have SEN, or might, in some cases, approaches to teaching and learning exacerbate their difficulties or discriminate against some learning styles?'

What concerns us here and in the next chapter is how learning theory can relate to us as teachers, and the learning environment we create for all the children in our class including those who have special educational needs. We need to have an understanding of the nature of teaching and learning if we are to make the classroom experience as effective as possible for the children within it. We also need to be open to fresh ideas and willing to address the challenges these may present to us.

> QtT S1.2, S1.7, S2.4, S3.1.3, S3.2.2, S3.3.1, S3.3.3, S3.3.4, S3.3.6, S3.3.8
>
> HLTA 1.2, 2.3, 2.5, 2.9, 3.3.1, 3.3.2, 3.3.5

Some influential theorists

As a starting point for considering learning theory in relation to special educational needs the work of Jean Piaget and Lev Vygotsky is particularly relevant.

Jean Piaget's work was particularly influential in the 1960s and 1970s. An aspect of his theory, and certainly one which contributed significantly to educational practice during the mid to late decades of the twentieth century, was his hypothesis of stages of development and 'learning readiness'. He suggested that children pass through various stages of development, and until they had passed through one, they would not be ready for the next.

The work of Vygotsky, a Soviet psychologist and historian, remains very influential and current. He saw learning as a largely social process that was at its most effective when the learner was involved with others. He also emphasised the importance of language and communication in the development of thinking and learning. Vygotsky explored the idea of building upon current knowledge and understanding with the help of others, which he referred to as 'scaffolding'. He developed the concept of the 'zone of proximal development', which can be thought of as the difference between what a learner can do on his/her own and that which he/she can do with the help of others.

There would be significant implications for the education of children and young people with special educational needs if one accepted:

1. that a child cannot move to the next stage until he/she is ready;

2. that language, communication and social interaction are vital elements in the development of a child's knowledge and understanding; and

3. that significant learning occurs through the process of 'scaffolding'.

The view that scaffolding can support further learning has considerable impact upon the role of the teacher. Rather than provide learning activities that match the learner's stage of development, the teacher stretches the learner by providing the help and support of someone with greater experience in the particular area. This empowers the teacher to take learning forward and build on what the learner already understands and uses. As an example, questions such as 'What if . . .?' or 'What would happen after . . .?' can be used to extend a learner's thinking no matter what level or stage he/she may have reached in independent terms. This opens up huge possibilities that may not have been perceived as likely if learning readiness was the sole gauge of a learner's current potential. If social interaction is an important element in learning, the learning environment must reflect this, and we see an example with the move from rows of desks to sitting around tables.

You are an experienced learner

Different approaches to learning suit different learners and different tasks. For example, how would you approach the memorising of a quote from a play in preparation for a literature examination? Secondly, what was, or might be, the most effective way for you to learn to reverse a car into a parking space? Your list might include some or all of the following:

Learning a quotation so that it can be memorised for an examination:

- repetition of the quote out loud or in your head with variations as to when and where this is most effective, e.g. just before sleeping, while pacing up and down, outside in the fresh air, lying down etc.;

- recording the quotation and playing it repeatedly – again there may be variations as to when and where this takes place, e.g. while driving or during exercise;

- visualising the quotation and 'seeing it in the mind's eye' when repeating it;

- writing the quotation out so as to separate it, visually, from the rest of the text;

- writing the quotation out repeatedly and saying it or 'hearing' it as you do so;

- writing the quotation out in different colours, e.g. for the key words;

- reading the quotation repeatedly after underlining key words;

- imagining or visualising the character saying the words in a context;

- persuading someone to test you and to prompt you when you hesitate;

- acting out the scene including the quotation; and

- using mnemonics.

Learning to reverse a car into a parking space:

- watching a demonstration on a video, DVD etc.;

- watching a demonstration by an instructor while you are a passenger;

- looking at a diagram or series of diagrams outlining the moves and then trying it yourself in the car;

- looking at a diagram or series of diagrams outlining the moves and then moving a model car through the movements on a model road before trying it yourself for real;

- carrying out the manoeuvre on a simulator;

- carrying out the manoeuvre while the instructor gives directions and instructions;

- reading a description of what to do, with or without an explanation as to why it is done this way;

- listening to a description of what to do, with or without the explanations above; and

- closing your eyes and visualising yourself executing the manoeuvre perfectly, before trying it in a car.

The first task, learning a quotation in preparation for an examination, is about finding the most effective way to memorise the quotation so that it can be recalled when required. The second is, in some respects, more complex. There is not only the question of memorising and recalling what needs to be done and in what sequence but also of learning the physical skills involved in performing this sequence.

The human brain

Our current knowledge about how the brain works is largely based on relatively recent research and this knowledge base is now impacting on learning theory. What is very clear is that we do not all process information in the same way. We have individual learning styles. The extent to which our personal learning style is inherent, is a matter of preference or is learnt is still very much a matter of debate, and Prashnig (1998) discusses this in some depth if you want to explore this further.

It has been recognised for some time that the two sides of the brain, the left and right hemispheres, have different processing styles. In broad terms, the left hemisphere seems to favour the logical and analytical while the right favours the more holistic and intuitive. Various lists of contrasting pairs have been drawn up by theorists in an attempt to describe these processing styles. Some of these are given below, together with examples of how these might manifest themselves in everyday tasks and activities. You might like to add other tasks and activities to the list.

Of course, for most of us it isn't as black and white as the contrasting pairs might suggest. While the approaches some people take to processing information are very left- or right-brain dominated, others have a flexibility which allows them to

Table 6.1 Left-brain and right-brain approaches

Left brain	Right brain	Example of the different approaches
Logical and analytical – looks at detail and parts of the whole	Intuitive and has an overview of the whole rather than details	Using a street map or 'following one's nose' in order to find way around a city
Linear	Holistic	Starting a jigsaw by looking at pieces and then putting them together or starting the jigsaw by looking at the picture and fitting the pieces together in relation to this (part to whole or whole to part)
Reality-based Keeps track of time	Fantasy-orientated Little sense of time	Rooted in reality and real life or uses imagination Good sense of time and the here and now or time and time limits seem meaningless Adapts to environment or changes environment to suit
Verbal and literal	Non-verbal and general	Can express self, describe actions and label or does and shows without the explanations
Structure	Integration	Directed, structured drawings and paintings or creative, non-representational drawings and paintings
Symbolic	Concrete	Think and learn with symbols (e.g. by reading) or think and learn by doing and touching (e.g. experimenting)
Sequential Sequences steps or tasks	Random	Makes a shopping list and goes through it step by step or picks things off the shelf as seen/thought of Follows a set of instructions/directions or adopts a random approach/starts in the middle
Functions include language, maths, logic, auditory processing, focus and concentration	Functions include the spatial, visual processing, music, rhythm, multi-tasking	

use both hemispheres more equally. As with special educational needs, there is a continuum. For further information and discussion see Prashnig (1998), who examines the research into the way the human brain works, and Portwood (2000), who also considers the research in specific relation to dyspraxia.

There is much evidence to suggest that the school environment largely favours those who are either left-brain dominant or who are flexible enough to integrate the use of both the left and right hemispheres. In spite of some shifts in recent years, many classrooms and teaching styles still largely favour the left-brain processors. Society places great emphasis on high academic standards which, in turn, are based on logic and rationality. Schools are encouraged to maintain high academic standards through, for example, testing, inspection and league tables. Intuition, creativity and sporting abilities are often not so highly prized by the establishment in general, although it is perhaps significant that the current heroes of the younger generation tend to be sporting personalities or those involved in the music or film industries. It is also significant that a number of such heroes confess to not having liked school or done very well academically.

Sensory preferences

Sensory preferences (often referred to as modalities) are key elements in our personal learning style. Four of the senses heavily influence intake of information and memory:

- seeing (visual)
- hearing (auditory)
- touching (tactile)
- whole-body feeling (kinaesthetic)

If we go back to the list of learning approaches, you will notice that some are visual and some are auditory with others involving both these sense modalities. Others are kinaesthetic, e.g. the act of writing and feeling the rhythm or flow of the words. What you will also be aware of, of course, is that different people use different channels in different circumstances. You may see and hear the acronym VAK (Visual, Auditory, Kinaesthetic) as a shorthand for this. Although it does not specifically include touching, you might like to mentally include this modality as Prashnig (see below) suggests.

One of the most obvious implications is that teachers need to take this into account by providing learning tasks that enable individual learners to use their sensory preferences and also develop other sensory pathways more fully. Another implication is that the teacher needs to present the lesson in a way that enables sensory preferences to be used by the learners. This will be discussed further in the next chapter but you may like to start thinking about how this might be done.

Prashnig (1998) also suggests that the sensory modalities develop in a specific order throughout the primary years – the kinaesthetic first, followed by tactile, visual and then, towards the end of KS2, auditory. This, she suggests, is why very young children learn by using their whole body and by touching.

You may find it useful to explore this a little further and to consider which sensory modalities, in your view, are made use of the most in 1. Foundation (Early Years), 2. KS1/2 and 3. KS3. Use the grid below and note which key stages the activity is likely to happen in and then note which modalities are used (it may be more than one): visual (V), auditory (A), tactile (T) or kinaesthetic (K).

Table 6.2 Use of sensory modalities

Activity	Key stage(s)	Sensory modalities (K,A,V,T)
Playing with sand or water	Foundation, KS1	T, K
Reading independently		
Writing up an experiment		
Learning a list of spellings		
Making music		
Mathematical computation		
Following a series of verbal instructions		
Listening to a story		
Drawing or painting		
Surfing the web for information		
Taking notes during the introduction to a new topic		
Swimming		
Taking digital photographs of an experiment		

The learning environment

Look back at the lists you made of approaches to memorising a quotation or learning to reverse a car into a parking space. Some of the approaches feature the environment or the way in which the environment is used by the learner, e.g. lying down to read or listening while driving or exercising. Some people like to learn in a quiet area while others prefer to do so with background music. Some prefer to be sitting upright in a bright light while others prefer more subdued lighting or a more relaxed position. Coloured paper, overlays or special lamps can help learners with dyslexia, and those on the autistic spectrum will prefer a quiet space with no distractions.

You might like to think about the environmental conditions in which you or your colleagues prefer to study. How do these compare with the approaches to study that have been suggested to you?

This brings us back to the question raised at the beginning of this chapter. Could it be that some children or young people who have been identified as having special educational needs have a learning style that is not catered for appropriately in their classroom? For some there may be a physical or sensory impairment or a medical condition which results in their needing specific equipment, resources or support in order for them to access most or all of the curriculum. Are there others whose learning styles are not those traditionally valued and who are therefore said to have learning or behavioural difficulties rather than alternative learning styles that could be catered for? The next chapter explores some teaching approaches that offer the potential for meeting the needs of more learners more of the time and could therefore be of benefit to some children and young people with SEN.

Revisiting classroom organisation and management

QtT S2.7, S3.3.7, S3.3.8

HLTA 2.9

If pupils have different learning styles, how can these be physically accommodated in a classroom? The primary classroom of today usually has different areas in the room for different tasks. There is usually a mat area where younger children can sit for class work or story time. Desk work is most commonly carried out while children are grouped around a table. There is frequently a 'quiet' area or reading corner. For younger children there are usually play areas such as the class shop or Wendy house, and sand and water areas. At least one computer is set up on a table or bench against one of the walls. There is some sort of board for writing on at the front of the class. There are drawers or trays for each child's work materials and others for class resources. Walls are covered with displays that celebrate, inform or, increasingly, are interactive. In other words, areas of the classroom are designated for particular types of task and activity and for storage.

A significant proportion of secondary classrooms are set out with traditional rows of tables or desks. However, increasingly this is changing, not least because of the greater amount of technology that is now to be found in many classrooms. Specialist areas may have fixed furniture, e.g. laboratory benches, which can limit the possibilities.

If, however, a classroom was arranged to take account of learning styles as well as types of learning activity, what difference might it make to the generalised picture of classrooms as described above? What might be the implications for classroom management if a classroom was arranged in this way?

Ideas about the learning environment may include some of the following:

- provision for alternative working positions, e.g. lying down to read or standing to write (have you noticed how some pupils seem to learn more effectively when standing up?);
- different lighting levels;
- headphones for background music, listening to a repeat of instructions etc.;
- availability of water and/or snacks;
- individual workstations as well as group tables;
- outdoor work areas with, for example, magnetic letter-boards on outside walls, sheltered reading/writing areas etc.;
- use of technology such as laptops and palmtops, which can provide freedom from working at a specific workstation;
- use of mobile phones or pagers for communication.

Among the implications would be the questions of:

- how, if at all, to group learners in the classroom;
- how to deploy the adults so as to ensure adequate supervision as well as input;
- how choices are made as to who works where and when and who makes them.

Approaches to grouping

In what ways have children or young people been grouped for teaching and learning purposes when you have been in the classroom? Why do you think they have been grouped in these ways and what are the advantages and disadvantages of these groupings? The grid below may help you to consider the options.

One of the biggest dangers for pupils with SEN is that they will be categorised as being of lower ability across much or even the whole of the curriculum. The mini case studies below of two children in the same class illustrate the potential difficulties.

Sheila and Jeremy may both be perceived as having SEN or as being low achievers or of low ability. However, their strengths and needs are very different in spite of the fact that both have difficulty with recording. If both are placed in the 'bottom' group or lower sets for much of the time, what might the implications be? Spend some time in considering this question before we explore it further in the next chapter.

JEREMY

Jeremy has a keen and passionate interest in football. He follows the football league closely on television, plays for a Sunday league team, for which he is captain, as well as for his school team and supports his local team by attending matches with his dad. Jeremy can tell you in great detail about matches he has seen and remembers scores and facts covering a number of years. Jeremy is also a strong swimmer and a keen athlete. He enjoys making models, drawing and painting (especially cartoons) and finding out, practically, how things work.

Jeremy has always found reading difficult and becomes very despondent about this as he would like to be able to follow newspaper reports about his team and get the level of information he wants from written material. He says that the words jump about after a while and he gets very tired when trying to read. He finds writing difficult too. Spelling is a major problem, and trying to get the right spellings leads to Jeremy 'loosing his flow'. He tends to write using the simplest words that he can and is unable to write for more than a few minutes at a time. If he manages more than three lines in a lesson his teacher thinks he has done very well. While Jeremy finds it difficult to record his learning in written form, he is able to talk about what he has done and achieved, and demonstrates a very high level of general knowledge.

SHEILA

Sheila is always the first to offer to help in the classroom and likes to have regular jobs. Once she has learnt how to do a routine task and has had a chance to practise, she is very reliable and takes a pride in a job well done. She particularly enjoys needlecraft and knitting and will sit for long periods of time at home totally engrossed in these activities.

Sheila can decode a passage quite well. There is very little expression in her reading and she can rarely explain what she has just read about. Although she has a good memory and can learn quite quickly by rote, her comprehension skills are poor. Her vocabulary is limited for her age and her spelling and writing skills are also below average. Sheila seldom asks for help if she is in difficulties but tends to struggle on until her difficulty is noticed. She has low self-esteem and describes herself as 'not being clever like the others'.

Figure 6.1 Case studies – Jeremy and Sheila

Table 6.3 Groupings

Grouping by ability, friendship etc.	Advantages	Disadvantages
Child or young person		
Teacher		

Grouping by ability	Advantages	Disadvantages
All those with SEN working together	Adult support can be targeted towards any pupil needing it because the supporter can stay at the one table all the time.	Needs vary enormously and may not be compatible. Work may not be differentiated appropriately.
Friendship groups	Friends may be more supportive.	Friends may not be the best workmates. Pupils may avoid choosing to work with those they don't know so well.
Learning style groups (similar or different learning styles together according to the task)	Learners work together and make a 'good team' with each contributing from a position of strength. Different strengths valued.	Takes more time to plan at first if teacher is not used to doing this. If grouping is not set up appropriately, those with SEN may become dispirited or be left out.
Those who have reached a similar stage in a particular piece of learning grouped together	Specific teaching can be provided. Effective use of time and resources.	Learners will not progress at same pace so those who progress more slowly may get left behind.

REFLECTION POINTS

At the beginning of this chapter, this question was raised:

Do all children who are failing at school and are also identified as having special educational needs really have SEN or might, in some cases, approaches to teaching and learning exacerbate their difficulties or discriminate against some learning styles?

What are your thoughts about this now? Do you have examples of when you have been able to modify teaching or learning strategies to enable a learner to make better use of his/her preferred learning styles? These may contribute towards evidence against some of the standards, e.g. HLTA 3.3.1, 3.3.2, 3.3.5 and QtT S3.1.1, S3.3.3, S3.3.4.

Teaching approaches

Individual learning styles and learning difficulties

We have seen the legal definition and we have briefly considered how difficult it is to actually define what a special educational need really is. There are clearly some learners whose needs are so great and complex that few would disagree that they have special needs; however, there are others who thrive in one learning environment but not another, pupils whose behaviour causes concern in one situation but who behave acceptably in another, and so on. In the last chapter, we questioned whether such learners who are failing to make progress have special educational needs or if the difficulty is rooted in the learning environment in which they find themselves. Once again there will be a continuum with some having both SEN *and* being in a learning environment that does not suit them.

In this chapter we will begin with two mini case studies. These are, of necessity, brief, and you will probably feel that you would like more information. However, in spite of this limitation, they are a good tool for the exploration of some of the areas we will be considering. As you read through the case studies 'Chris' and 'Suki', you might like to note your own response and attitude to their needs, and then, as you read through the rest of the chapter, consider if and how any of the approaches explored might support their learning.

CHRIS – YEAR 2

Teacher – Mrs Daniels: Chris is unable to sit still for more than a minute or two. He fidgets and fiddles constantly, often touching other children or their belongings. Literacy Hour is a nightmare with mat work almost impossible because of Chris's constant moving about and touching things he shouldn't. He finds most lessons very difficult and rarely completes any written work. The one thing that he does enjoy is drama and he is good at that as long as he can do his own thing. He doesn't like being told how to play a character or what to do on stage so I daren't let him have a lead part for parents' assembly, for example. I don't know how he will cope in Key Stage 2. He will have to learn to sit still and be quiet then.

Chris's mum: Chris is a loving little boy. He is very curious and loves to explore new environments. We take him camping and he loves the freedom to run about and explore. He knows all about wildlife and tells us the names of trees and birds. He is so excited when he finds out more and loves to go to the library with his dad to look up about a bird or animal he has seen while we have been away. Chris also goes to a drama club. This seems to channel his energies. He is very lively and boisterous sometimes but loves going to the club. They do all sorts of things and really encourage the kids to make suggestions and try new things out. He is full of it when he comes home.

We are really worried about Chris at school. He doesn't enjoy going and seems to get told off every five minutes. I dread going to the gate to meet him in case his teacher takes the opportunity to tell me how naughty he has been again. I just don't know what to do about it. His teacher says he should see the Educational Psychologist but his dad won't hear of it. He says that there is nothing wrong with Chris that a good teacher or a good hiding wouldn't sort out.

Chris: I hate school. Mrs Daniels doesn't like me. When I go into class she always says that she hopes I will be a good boy, not like yesterday. There are lots of things for us to look at but we mustn't touch them. There are lots of books too. We have to sit still and be quiet, but I can't. I don't like being knocked by other kids. I like to spread out. I don't like sitting on the mat unless I sit behind Becky. She has long silky hair and I like to put plaits in it.

Chris's friend – Jack: Chris is funny. He makes me laugh. School is boring unless Chris is there. Mrs Daniels keeps telling him off but he is still naughty. She says he must keep his hands and feet to himself – it is one of our classroom rules. We go to drama club together and Chris is brilliant. He has lots of ideas. I think he will be a famous actor when he grows up.

SUKI – YEAR 6

Teacher – Mr Bowman: Suki came to this school six months ago when her family moved down from the north. She is very good at problem solving and thinking skills. Streets ahead of most of the class. I have difficulty getting her to write things down properly though. She much prefers to draw diagrams and charts or to make notes rather than writing in proper sentences. English isn't her first language so this might have something to do with it, although her spoken English is excellent and very fluent. Her last school didn't seem to think written work was a problem.

Suki is easily bored – she is impatient to get on and take things further. This causes some problems as she doesn't suffer fools gladly and frequently falls out with others in the class if they are not so quick. She isn't a team player really – she much prefers to work on her own. Having said that, she also likes the other children to comment favourably about her work and she seems to thrive on praise.

Suki's father: Suki is very bright and we have high hopes for her. Both my wife and I are solicitors and, who knows, perhaps Suki will follow suit. She has always been very self-sufficient, unlike her two sisters, although we do worry that she hasn't many friends – not real friends anyway. She prefers adult company; she always has, even when she was very little.

Suki: School is OK. Mr Bowman gives me some really interesting things to do sometimes although he wants me to write everything out in detail and I think that is a waste of time. If notes or a diagram says what you want it to, why write pages about it? I especially hate drafting and redrafting. I love Science, Maths and D&T, especially experiments. Sometimes Mr Bowman gives me a really hard problem to solve, which is great. He says I am better than he is at science.

Jemma (sits at Suki's table): Suki is strange really. She gets really cross if we don't do what she wants in class but she is ever so clever. If she is in our group for something like Science we leave her alone to get on with the hard things and then she tells us the answers. She always finishes before the rest of us. She doesn't seem to like music or clothes or anything like that so you can't chat with her at lunchtime or have a laugh with her or anything like that.

Figure 7.1   Case studies – Chris and Suki

Teaching approaches

We have already explored some of the factors that contribute to effective learning and teaching and, in particular, we have begun to consider the diversity of learning styles and approaches to teaching and learning. It is clear that in order to be effective a teacher must be able to respond to the diversity of the learning styles and needs of all his/her pupils. In this section we will be considering some approaches which aim to do this. As you read the chapter, think about the approaches that you use already but also consider ways in which you could develop other approaches in order to meet the learning needs of the wider class. Use any opportunities you have to observe other teachers and teaching assistants.

Multi-sensory teaching

Any teaching which requires the learner to use more than one sensory channel could be said to be multi-sensory. An effective teacher will present content using different sensory channels and will also allow pupils to use the different channels for recording, reporting, communicating and learning. Ruth Kershaw discusses this and the implications for the learning environment in chapter 2 of Whitebread (2000).

However, in SEN terms, the expression 'multi-sensory teaching' is most frequently used to mean a specific method of teaching reading and spelling through using a number of senses simultaneously, thus enabling the child to memorise more effectively. It is usually recommended as part of a structured programme. The major sensory channels we are referring to here are the auditory, visual, oral, tactile and kinaesthetic.

O'Connell (1994) gives an example of multi-sensory teaching with a breakdown of the teaching steps for learning the initial sound 'd'. A condensed overview follows:

1. Trace round the outline of a plastic 'd' while looking at the shape and saying the letter name and sound. (This may be modelled by the teacher first.)

2. Say the letter name/sound and write from memory.

Not only does this ensure that all these channels are used at the same time but it also ensures that the child is able to form the connection between the shape, sound and writing of letters (or indeed any other symbols such as numbers). This aids memory and also makes use of a child's stronger sensory channels to help support the weaker ones. Try the steps above for yourself so you get a feel for how this works.

The example uses a plastic letter 'd' as a tactile resource. Think of some other resources that could provide for the tactile and kinaesthetic channels to be used in the learning of the initial sound 'd'.

Once you begin thinking about this, you will be able to come up with lots of ideas. Some possibilities could be:

● writing in sand or salt with a finger or stick;

● using a 'd' made of other materials, e.g. wood, or a textured 'd' made of velvet, dried PVA glue or string (remember that the child may be tracing the letter with his/her finger so avoid uncomfortable textures like coarse sandpaper);

> **TIP**
>
> *Wherever possible, use 3D shapes that cannot be reversed. Some letters look similar to others when reversed (e.g. b and d; n and u) but those which, for example, are painted on one side or are moulded so that they are smooth on just the one side will help to avoid some of the reversing problems many children have.*

- on a larger scale – on a beach or in a large sandpit – the shapes can be drawn with a rake or a comb;
- a large 'd' chalked on a playground can be walked around (or even hopped or skipped) instead of finger-traced;
- a letter 'd' can be formed with the fingers;
- a letter 'd' can be traced on another's back or back of the hand; or
- the letter can be written in the air ('sky-writing').

Some of these ideas will prove useful in whole-class work in the primary phase, e.g. literacy or numeracy sessions. One of the potential difficulties of having a whole class sitting and waiting while, for example, one child comes up to the front to write a 'd' on the whiteboard or flipchart is that the non-involved children will probably misbehave. The teacher needs to have activities to keep children engaged in these circumstances. Having the whole class sky-writing a 'd', for example, while one child is at the front, enables all to remain involved and the teacher to see if any child is experiencing particular problems.

> **TIP**
>
> *Remember that if you are facing the children and 'sky-writing' a 'd' for them, it will be in reverse. Either turn round so your back is to them (but looking over your shoulder) or learn to sky-write in reverse. The latter takes practice to get it both right and smoothly executed. Don't be tempted to try it without practice.*

Keeping an ideas bank of multi-sensory activities and ways of presenting new ideas/tasks or materials, and adding to it as you think of, see or hear about other activities, can be very useful. Some of the ideas already suggested might be a good starting point and some more ideas for you to explore follow:

- Use of rhymes or chants for, e.g., learning tables, days of the week etc. These can be powerful learning tools but when sensory channels are used in addition to auditory they become even more effective.
- Explaining how a calculation is done while drawing what is happening in diagram form or (for simpler calculations with smaller numbers) using plastic cubes or counters. Use of colour can add to this, e.g. different coloured counters for the different elements of the calculation or for tens and units, or digits before and after the decimal point.

These examples have an obvious primary phase application but the principles apply equally to older learners, including adults. Many teachers of dyslexic children and adults would feel that the multi-sensory approaches developed over the last forty or so years are the most effective ways to support the learning of reading and spelling. Both Ott (1997) and Townend and Turner (2000) describe multi-sensory teaching in detail, and both these books are also recommended for detailed and in-depth discussion about dyslexia and how to manage it.

At the beginning of this section on multi-sensory approaches I expressed the view that an effective teacher will present content using different sensory channels and will also allow pupils to use the different channels for recording, reporting, communicating and learning. Advances in technology and its use in classrooms have given teachers and teaching assistants a far wider range of resources for doing this, e.g.:

- use of search engines on the internet to find information;
- interactive whiteboards and projectors;
- digital cameras and camcorders;
- use of voting pads such as Quizdom (see the Resources section under ICT);
- video-conferencing or the use of the potentially more flexible webcams; and
- radio projectors linked to tablet laptops so that every learner can interact with the materials at his/her desk rather than having to come out to the front.

Multi-sensory approaches are highly effective for all learners and the previous chapter will have given you a number of suggestions as to why this should be. A good teacher makes use of all the sensory channels as well as using sensory language that resonates with the preferred sensory channels of the learners.

Accelerated learning

Unlike multi-sensory teaching, the term 'accelerated learning' has not come to be perceived as an approach mainly for children with SEN. Alastair Smith (1996) suggests that accelerated learning is 'learning how to make learning more likely'. In other words, accelerated learning is not an 'off-the-shelf' scheme of work or a scripted teaching technique but rather a pulling together of practical strategies for effective learning based on the most up-to-date knowledge and understanding that we have about how the brain functions. All children are seen as having individual learning preferences and needs, so in that sense accelerated learning resonates well with the concept of the inclusive classroom. There is a growing move towards embracing accelerated learning strategies and concepts and you are likely to see evidence of this when you visit and work in schools during your course. There are some excellent books, including those by Smith, on the market which provide both underpinning theory and lots of practical strategies for use in the classroom. This section can only be a brief taster but it is hoped it might encourage you to find out more.

Accelerated learning could be seen as taking an even more holistic approach to learning than multi-sensory approaches, since learning environment, resources, planning and delivery are all taken into account and it is not designed primarily for a particular group of learners. However, the two approaches are not mutually exclusive, and you will be aware of common strands and common thinking. The main characteristics of accelerated learning follow, together with the QtT and HLTA standards they most obviously relate to:

● Lesson planning and delivery which takes into account all learners' needs (QtT S3.3.3, S3.3.4, S3.3.6, S3.3.7, HLTA 3.3.3).

● An open and relaxed state for different activities, e.g. learning, revision, energy.

● High teacher expectations (QtT S3.3.1, S3.3.9, HLTA 1.1).

● Effective teaching through visual, auditory and kinaesthetic channels.

● A variety of teaching and learning strategies that meet the diversity of learning needs in the classroom (QtT S3.3.1, S3.3.4, S3.3.5, S3.3.6, HLTA 3.1.2).

● Building and maintaining self-esteem (QtT S3.3.6, HLTA 3.3.1).

● Encouraging children to try, test and review (QtT S3.2.2, HLTA 3.2.2).

Lesson planning and delivery

I would not expect you to find that the accelerated learning cycle is at odds with any input you may have received about lesson planning and delivery and, for many readers, such inputs will have included the accelerated learning cycle anyway. However, I suggest that you consider this next section alongside any inputs you may have received and, in particular, how the cycle might help to enhance your learning about lesson planning.

Smith *et al.* (2003) suggest a four-stage cycle with the learner and learning as the focus.

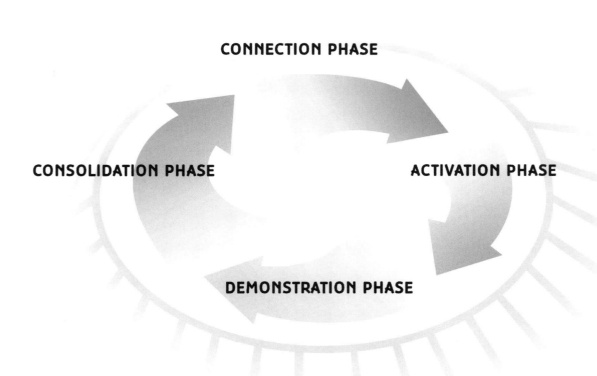

Figure 7.2 Smith *et al.*'s four-stage Cycle of Learning (from *Accelerated Learning: A User's Guide*, 2003, Network Educational Press)

At first glance the stages in the cycle may look much the same as more traditional approaches to lesson planning, but the real emphasis here is on the learner and what needs to be done to ensure that the learning that takes place is as successful as possible. The 'connect' stage is not merely a question of saying what was done in the last lesson and what is going to be done in this one, in the hope that this will be significant to all the children; it is about making learning personal so that each child understands the big picture, so the picture must be made meaningful for each individual. The use of sensory language; providing brief activities which enable individuals or pairs to describe what they already know about the topic or to relate it to their own; personal learning goals; and creating a mind map are all possible approaches. From personal experience I have found that building up a map or display linking aspects of a topic as it is worked through to be extremely effective for everyone in the classroom (including the volunteer who came in for one morning a week and could then quickly see what had been covered or discovered since her last visit). Similarly, a map or diagram of what is to be covered in the future and how it links to other topics can be an important support tool.

You will probably be familiar with the idea of learning outcomes and ensuring children are aware of these. It is more than putting these outcomes on the board and telling the pupils what they are; each pupil needs to be able to make sense of the outcomes and relate them to their own learning goals. The content therefore needs to be broken down into small-enough segments and to be differentiated appropriately.

As you will appreciate, the 'connect' stage takes some planning and thought and is not merely covered by 'This is what we did last week; today we are doing this and the outcomes are a, b and c'. You may feel that the most important part of the lesson is the 'activate' stage, but attention to the connect stage will ensure that children are prepared to learn. Often all that is required is two or three minutes of focused activity in order for that preparation to be successful.

Using multi-sensory language will be crucial at the 'activation' stage as will a variety of inputs so that there is the opportunity for all or most sensory modalities to be utilised and for children to be actively involved. For further discussion of the use of sensory language, see O'Connor (2001) and Smith (1996).

You might like to spend a few minutes exploring the idea of sensory language or adding some more examples to the grid below.

Learners should be aware of what constitutes success for that particular activity. Over time, activities should utilise and balance the seven intelligences (linguistic, mathematical, visual & spatial, musical, interpersonal, intrapersonal and kinaesthetic). For further information about the seven intelligences see Gardner (1993) or Smith (1996).

Table 7.1 Sensory language

Visual	Auditory	Kinaesthetic
I see what you mean	I like the sound of that	I feel out of touch
Can you picture the scene?	That rings a bell	Time is running out
Seeing eye to eye	On the same wavelength	Surfing the net

Demonstration and consolidation are sometimes seen as being one and the same. Accelerated learning differentiates between the two. The 'demonstration' stage is the opportunity for the individual to show what has been understood while the 'consolidation' stage provides the child with the opportunity to learn techniques of memory recall and retention and to consolidate his/her learning. Providing safe ways for a child to demonstrate understanding is vital if anxiety is to be avoided and learning is to remain fun.

Creating an effective learning environment

QtT S3.3.1, S3.3.8

HLTA 3.3.5, 3.3.8

It may seem obvious that the classroom needs to be appropriately arranged to facilitate the learning that is to take place. However, this is not always the case and it is well worth taking the time to make sure that the classroom layout is as supportive of learning as possible. In the last chapter, for example, we considered ways in which children might be grouped for different learning activities. If we are going to be flexible enough to enable groupings to change, the classroom layout must be flexible to accommodate this without the need for major furniture moving. Colour, smell, warmth, fresh air, the availability of drinking water and music can all contribute towards effective conditions for learning.

Creating an appropriate mood or state for learning is part of creating an effective learning environment. Effective learning does not take place if the learner is anxious or stressed, so creating an appropriate state to start with is crucial. Relaxation exercises, Brain Gym® and positive posters/displays at eye level are all ways of doing this.

Smith (1996) describes Brain Gym® as 'a physical activity which connects left and right brain and is useful for managing the "state" of learners'. It was created by Paul Dennison specifically to help youngsters with SEN but has come to be seen as a valuable tool for all learners. One of the most well-known Brain Gym activities is sky-writing the sign for infinity (a sideways figure of eight). Smith suggests doing it with each hand in turn for three circuits and then by clasping the hands together with the thumbs pointing upwards for a further three. He refers to it as 'lazy eights' in Smith (1996), where you will also find other Brain Gym® activities.

Music is also a powerful creator of state. Research suggests that a brainwave pattern of 60–70 beats per minute, known as the 'alpha state', is the most effective state for learning. Listening to music that has a similar number of beats per minute can help to encourage the 'alpha state', which is why music is such a prominent feature of accelerated learning. Baroque music, e.g. Bach, and the music of Mozart, in particular, frequently has 60–70 beats per minute so this explains why you may have heard in the press and elsewhere that Mozart's music is good for the brain. There are also compilations of specially composed modern music with 60–70 beats per minute. At other times you will want learners to be in a more energised or relaxed state and the choice of appropriate music can assist in this too.

You might like to start making a list of music that would be suitable for a variety of situations in school, e.g. coming into or leaving assembly on a 'normal' day; a SATs day/end of term etc., to relax or to energise your class. There are some suggestions for music to use in the classroom in Smith (1996).

Make a note (preferably with diagrams) of any Brain Gym® activities you come across. Try them out with colleagues before using them in class so you know you can do them fluently. Some sound easy but actually take practice.

Self-esteem and self-confidence

We will be thinking about your own self-esteem as a teacher or teaching assistant in Chapter 8, although many of the principles and ideas that follow will be equally applicable to you as to the learners in your class. Why is self-esteem so important? When self-esteem is poor, learning is less effective. The learner who has a positive belief in him/herself and feels valued is more likely to be able to set appropriate goals and learn new skills and knowledge. Many readers will know this from their own experience.

Building self-esteem is one of the pillars of accelerated learning and Smith (1996) suggests the BASIS model for the enhancement of self-esteem/self-belief:

Belonging – the need to be valued, recognised etc.

Aspirations – a belief that there is a purpose to learning

Safety – a safe environment is one in which the learner feels secure enough to take learning risks

Identity – 'accurate self-knowledge'; a sense of individuality

Success – regular and positive feeling of achievement

Figure 7.3   BASIS model for self-esteem

The brief section on accelerated learning will have highlighted the importance of self-esteem for successful learning. Those with SEN or other particular individual needs such as EAL can be seen as being particularly vulnerable to feelings of self-doubt and low self-esteem, although many children and adults might appear to have many disadvantages and difficulties in comparison with their peers, yet have a real sense of self-worth and a very positive attitude.

Conversely, there are those who would appear to have every reason to be positive and to have high self-esteem, yet who are plagued by self-doubt and a negative attitude. However, the classroom environment and culture can serve to raise or lower self-esteem regardless of how high or low it may be in the first place. You might like to look back at the two mini case studies and consider how both Chris and Suki might fare on the BASIS model and what might be done to build their self-esteem in the classroom. It is also important to remember that low self-esteem does not always manifest itself in withdrawn and depressed behaviour or anxiety; some of the most seemingly confident people can have a poor self-concept.

Drawing on pupils' experiences (QtT 3.3.6) can be one way of enhancing self-esteem. It demonstrates that the teacher cares about the individual child and his/her feelings, it fosters a sense of individuality and identity and confirms that the child is valued. If we go back to Chris, for example, it is clear that there are two areas of interest and experience that could provide excellent starting points for his class teacher. One is his evident interest in wildlife and the other is his interest in drama.

The use of approaches such as circle time are also extremely effective at building a sense of belonging, safety and success for the class as a whole as well as for each individual child. The group or class work in a circle and to agreed rules enables all to feel safe and valued and to have a fair share of 'turns'. The activities or games are designed to allow all to be equally valued; to gel and to learn about each other's strengths, weaknesses and interests; to promote positive attitudes and trust; and to develop thinking skills and a team spirit. A regular circle session is well worth the time taken from the rest of the very crowded timetable. There are many books about circle time with lots of ideas for activities and games. As a starting point, those with suggested sequences of activities for different age groups are probably the best to start with so that you build up your own experience of putting together a programme. Any of the books published by Lucky Duck or written by Jenny Mosley are useful starting points.

Feedback, including marking, is a very important element of maintaining or enhancing self-esteem. Think about the purpose of, for example, marking a particular piece of work and how you want the learner to respond. Remember that the message is only as good as the interpretation the child or young person makes. It will hardly be an incentive if a learner interprets your comment or mark as indicating that he/she is no good at maths or spelling. QtT Standard 3.2.2 is particularly relevant here. If you are one of the many who feel that they cannot do maths, draw or sing in tune, you might like to think back to what reinforced your view. I would think it highly likely that what you perceived (rightly or wrongly) as negative feedback or criticism from teachers, family or friends contributed to your feelings of poor self-worth in the subject in question.

Drawing up a menu of ways of providing feedback and celebrating success can be worthwhile and also helps to keep your responses to achievement, effort and success fresh and original. Some of the following may give you a start, but remember the golden rules of rewards – they must be appropriate to the child, contingent (i.e. dependent upon achieving a specified target or goal) and as immediate as possible (especially for the younger child):

● Boaster posters – a large sheet displayed prominently in the primary classroom on which successes are recorded. These can be very simple, e.g. *Phillip played with Nathan today*, if Phillip needs a lot of encouragement to play with other children, or *Tracey has learnt her 3 times table*. To start with, it is probably best if the adults put things up on the boaster poster but children can be encouraged to make suggestions about others in the class or even write things up themselves. If they have been used to accelerated learning and/or circle time, they will soon develop the skills to do this. Once learners are used to setting their own targets and being realistic about them, they can also produce their own boaster posters and/or mind maps as a record of their achievements and progress. A similar strategy can also be used equally effectively in the secondary setting.

A more visual presentation is more effective for many learners (and their parents/carers) than a written report:

● Charlie Charts for individual, group or class use – there are a huge variety of charts to colour in, section by section, as goals are reached, and these are very commonly used in primary schools. An individualised one that matches a child's interests can be very effective. A similar idea can be used with a jigsaw or other picture cut into pieces after mounting on card. Each time the child achieves a specified goal/target, he/she gets another piece of the jigsaw. Make sure the child knows exactly what has to be done to achieve the next piece.

- A class picture which is added to – I have used this very effectively with, for example, a Christmas scene. Pieces for the scene are prepared beforehand and when a child achieves something special, he/she is invited to add a piece to the picture or tableau. In the case of the Christmas scene this included sheep and other animals, stars, the shepherds, angels and the stable. A colleague did something similar with a class tree. In the spring, the children added small, light green leaves; in the summer they replaced these with larger, deeper leaves; in the autumn, appropriately coloured leaves were added; and at Christmas the tree was bare of leaves but had decorations added instead. Each leaf or decoration had the child's name on it and what he/she had done to receive it.

Personal teaching style

Prashnig (1998) suggests that 'we tend to teach in the same way we like to learn'. You might like to consider how far you think this is true. There is little doubt, however, that there will be those in your class who will like to learn in a similar way to you. Equally, there will be those who do not like to learn in the way you do or for whom your way will be less effective. If you teach in the same way that you like to learn you are going to miss the mark for at least some of the children or young people in your care. The answer is to deploy a variety of teaching styles; you are more likely to get it right for more of the learners more of the time.

REFLECTION POINTS

The following suggestions provide starting points for further discussion.

1. List ways a learner can demonstrate his/her new understanding. Some possibilities might be producing a booklet or mind map individually or in pairs, telling or showing the class, role play and quizzes.

2. What are you able to say about Chris and Suki as learners from these brief case studies? Do you feel that either or both have special educational needs? If you were their teacher, what do you think you could do to meet their needs and enable them to use their preferred learning styles? If you are working with older children, consider the possible scenarios for teaching an older 'Chris' or 'Suki' when he/she moves into Year 7.

3. This chapter has provided a very brief view of some teaching approaches for the inclusive classroom. In what ways are they similar to or different from the approaches to teaching and learning you experienced (a) when at school yourself and (b) during your teacher or teaching assistant training? What might have made your own learning even more successful?

4. In what ways, if any, has your attitude to the needs of children with SEN who are gifted and talented or for whom English is an additional language changed as a result of considering inclusive approaches such as accelerated learning?

CHAPTER 8

School-based training and preparing for qualified status

In this chapter SEN and related issues are considered in the context of school experience and preparation for qualified status.

The common threads for all trainee teachers are that:

- it is in school that you will begin to work directly with learners with a wide range of needs including SEN; and

- regardless of the route or course you are embarking upon, you will be required to provide evidence that you have reached QTS standards because there are a number of practical-based standards that can only be demonstrated through actually working with children or young people.

Similarly, those looking to meet the professional standards for HLTA status will also be gathering evidence for this while working in a school setting.

Time spent on school placements is exciting and challenging but can also be very stressful for a trainee teacher, so you need to make the best possible use of your time. Make sure that you are familiar with the standards before you start, and look for ways of demonstrating that you have made progress towards, or reached any of, them. You will need to provide evidence for this so be sure that you know what your ITT provider expects from you in this regard. You may, for example, be asked to cross-reference your lesson plans or evaluations by referring to specific standards. This is where familiarity with the standards will help enormously.

Making the most of your time in school

The reality of teaching a class of children or young people really hits home when you are in the classroom. It is there that you see that learners do not fit into neat little boxes or categories. There may, for example, be a number who have reading difficulties or for whom English is an additional language, but each will be different and will have different strengths, interests and needs. Being on a school placement gives you a chance to observe how different pupils respond to different teaching approaches, tasks and methods of support.

Visits and placements in schools

Visits and placements can take a number of forms depending on your course and the stage you have reached in your training. Initial visits, especially on a three- or four-year undergraduate course, may be largely awareness-raising and familiarising experiences in which observation and discussion feature more strongly than working directly with children. The suggestions for focused observation in the next section may help you to make the most of such experiences. However, for most trainee teachers, and certainly for those on the employment-based routes and Postgraduate Certificate in Education (PGCE) courses, it is more likely to be a case of being in at the deep end at a very early stage. There simply is not the time for a gentle lead in. Your final placement, of course, will be the one where you teach 'a class or classes over a sustained and substantial period of time' and demonstrate that you are able 'to teach across the age and ability range' for which you are trained. You will also want to feel that you are making a positive difference to the children and young people you work with.

QtT S3.3.11

Early visits to placement schools

Your ITT provider will give you guidance as to what to find out about and how to prepare for placements. Most allocate preliminary visits of some sort where you will get to know relevant teachers and other members of staff, gather information about the school and the pupils, agree your timetable etc. This is a good time, even if you are not required to do so, to ask to see the school's policies for SEN, behaviour, bullying and equal opportunities. These will tell you a lot about the school, its values, its ethos and the quality of relationships it aspires to. Admittedly, any policies are only as good as their implementation, but looking at the policies is a good starting point and can also be an excellent basis for discussion. As you experience placements in different schools you will begin to 'get a feel' for what makes an effective policy and what to look out for when seeking your first post as an NQT.

These early visits are also a time for finding out more about the children and young people you will be working with on your placement. Again your ITT provider will give guidance. However, it is also worthwhile thinking about what information you feel that you need in order to 1. prepare for the placement and 2. establish a positive working relationship with pupils as rapidly as possible. You do not have a lot of time to do this, especially on a five- or six-week placement. The information that you have identified as most helpful will probably include:

- what pupils have covered;
- what they are able to do;
- what they are still finding difficult or need further help with; and
- particular strengths, interests and needs of individual learners, including those on the special needs register (at School Action and School Action Plus).

Some of the last can be found effectively through focused observation (see below) and spending time with the children including at lunchtimes and playtimes or, with older pupils, in homework clubs and extra-curricular activities. Time spent with pupils will also enable you to start establishing a positive relationship, but do remember that there is a difference between taking a genuine interest as part of a professional relationship and being a chum. You need to maintain your authority.

You will probably have included the teacher's records of pupils' progress in your list of documents to look at. You may well find that teachers use a different format to the ones you have been shown before but this is another good opportunity to see how different systems work. It is also a chance to explore how useful records are and how much is needed in order to plan effectively.

Did you include IEPs in your list? As we have seen, an IEP should be a teaching and learning plan which is comprehensible to staff and parents and is a working document. School placements provide the perfect opportunity to see IEPs in action. If IEPs are as effective as they should be, they will be a real help in ensuring continuity and progress for the pupils who have them. If the IEPs are comprehensible to staff and parents, they should certainly be comprehensible to you and should help you in your planning.

One of the potential problems with gathering information about the learners in the class is the issue of expectation. If you are told that Susan is very disruptive or that Ranjit does not listen, how will this affect the way you interact with these pupils? If you assume that Susan is going to be difficult, how will this come across to Susan and how might she respond? Behaviour is one of the most problematic areas in this respect. Your teacher may tell you about a learner for whom acceptable classroom behaviour can be problematic or who is, in some way, difficult to teach. How will you respond to this and what information is helpful? Knowing how the pupil usually responds to particular situations or what appear to be trigger points may be useful, whereas a long list of misdemeanours may not. Also bear in mind that behaviour is contextual and a pupil may respond very differently to you (possibly more positively) than to the usual class teacher.

Classroom observation

It is a real privilege to be in another teacher's classroom, especially if the teacher is an excellent practitioner. It is a wonderful opportunity to watch and question, but focused observation is much more valuable than just sitting and watching.

QtT S3.1.1

HLTA 1.6

The very basic proforma (Figure 8.1) can be used for focus on an individual child or on several and can be adapted to suit different circumstances. The top gives space for general background information so you can, for example, indicate the size of the class or group, role of adults in the classroom, structure of the lesson, classroom environment etc., as appropriate. Two columns are provided underneath. The right-hand column is for your factual notes of what you observed. The left-hand column is for context so that you can record changes in lesson structure or times. Figure 8.2 gives an illustration of an observation sheet.

Some suggestions for possible foci are outlined below:

1. Focus on a particular learner:
   - When given a new task/activity, how does the learner respond?, e.g. starts straight away, needs adult reassurance or clarification before starting, seeks clarification or reassurance from peers, appears unable or unwilling to start etc. Don't forget to make a note of the activity and how it is presented (you can do this in the left-hand column of the proforma) because you may well find that the learner's response changes with different activities or if a task

Class/group:	Lesson:
Date:	
Teacher/teaching assistants and other adults:	
Context/background:	
Focus for the observation:	

Context	Observation

Figure 8.1   Basic classroom observation proforma

is presented in another way. Are you able to draw any conclusions about the most or least effective ways of presenting a new task to this learner?

- Make a note of the various ways in which the learner is asked to, and actually does, record his/her learning. Are there some ways the learner seems to prefer or finds more difficult?, e.g. writing independently, copying, drawing pictures or diagrams, making an audio recording, word processing, using symbols of some sort, model making, drawing a chart, completing a drawn chart etc.

2. Focus on three or four pupils from different groups. This will enable you to compare learning styles, responses etc. of several learners in the same setting:

- You could use the suggestions for focusing on an individual pupil but you can also now consider how to compare responses. This can give a good insight into different learning styles and needs. Follow this up by thinking about how you could make best use of the diversity of responses and also enable all learners to approach the task with confidence. Think how you could maximise on this if you were the teacher.

3. Focus on the teacher. It would be courteous to explain to the teacher what you would like to do and why, and, if possible, try to arrange a time when you can have a discussion with the teacher afterwards. This will give you a valuable insight into the reasons for the approaches taken. Take care not to come across

Class/group: 7K   Lesson: English

Date: 3rd March 2005

Teacher/teaching assistants and other adults: AL (English teacher), RB (teaching assistant)

Context/background: Introduction to a new text

Focus for the observation:

Three pupils identified for the observation with help of English teacher –
Colin, Simone and Sara.
Colin has some difficulties with written work.
English is not Simone's first language – she has better oral than written English.
Sara is of average ability.
Focus is to be on the responses of each of these pupils to the introduction of the new text and to the tasks set for this lesson.
Follow-up discussion afterwards with teacher and learning mentor re. what I have found out about their responses and learning styles.

Context	Observation
Teacher puts learning outcomes on the board and explains these as he goes	Colin groans, RB sitting close by but moves to sit nearer Colin. Simone appears to be listening intently. Sara writes the LOs down.
Pupils asked to work in pairs to tell each other if they know anything about the book, have read it before or seen the film	Colin asks RB if it is OK just to talk and to check he doesn't have to write anything down. He hasn't seen the film or read the book but appears more interested when his partner and RB tell him that it is set in the town where Colin used to live.
Feedback to class	Simone talks to her partner about seeing the film and describes a particularly vivid scene.
	Sara has already read the book as has her partner and they discuss whether they would like to see the film or not.

Figure 8.2 A part completed example

as being judgemental or critical and take time to prepare your questions carefully:

- How does he/she present a new topic? How does he/she ensure that all the class/group are able to show what they have learnt and understood?

- What forms of differentiation has the teacher used? How has the teacher used ICT? How does the teacher record progress during and after the lesson?

- Possible questions/discussion points for after the lesson:

  (a) I noticed that you asked the children to . . . [work in pairs, choose their own partners/group, work on their own, watch the video all the way through before asking questions etc.]. Why did you decide upon that rather than . . .?

  (b) Some of the pupils were . . . [working on their own, working with the LSA, using the computer etc.]. How did you decide who would be doing what?

  (c) How do you keep a record of progress when . . . [children have been working on computer(s) or discussing work together or with another adult]?

Planning for differentiation and evaluation

Effective differentiation is the main way of supporting children with SEN. You might like to consider to what extent you, and teachers you have worked with, see the differences in the abilities and learning styles of pupils in the class as problems to be resolved, as an asset or both. McNamara and Moreton (1997) have some interesting ideas and discuss this further. Differentiation can involve consideration of type of teacher input; tasks and activities; expected outcomes; pace and timing; appropriate (perhaps adapted) resources; level of adult/peer support. An important issue when planning support in a lesson is one of encouraging independence.

Strategies you might consider, depending on the age and needs of the learner, could be:

- Break tasks or activities down into chunks, then consider which chunks the child can do unaided, which with some help and which independently. Plan support accordingly.

- Ask the child or young person what he/she would like to do or try to do with or without assistance.

- Establish a system or code for the learner to indicate when support or help is needed so it does not have to be offered by the teacher or teaching assistant every time. In other words give some or all control over support to the child or young person.

- Encourage independence by encouragement, recognition of progress and expressions of confidence.

It is very important to establish systems to ensure that whoever is supporting the child/young person records what is done with assistance, some assistance or none at all, and make sure this is accessible to all involved.

From time to time you are likely to have pupils in your class who have more severe and/or complex needs. Establishing what support is available, building a good relationship with parents and other professionals involved and working closely with your SENCO will be key.

Behavioural needs, particularly where there is unpredictability, severity, frequency of disturbance or potential safety issues, are often the most difficult to manage even for the more experienced teacher. Other needs which, for example, mean a reorganisation of the classroom to accommodate equipment, can also have a very significant impact on how the classroom can be managed. Again, you will be working with what you have and, hopefully, reminding yourself frequently of the positives, e.g.:

- when there has been a breakthrough or a small step in progress (remember to record it);

- when a reorganisation of furniture or resources has been an improvement;

- when child X has only shouted out eight times rather than the ten times, as yesterday, or when Y has been attentive or engrossed (even if only for a matter of seconds);

- positive responses towards you, other colleagues, other children from the pupil or parents.

Reframing can help you with this too. If you begin to think in the negative, turn it round so it becomes positive, e.g. 'Linda sat still for five minutes during the story today', rather than, 'Linda was wandering around for most of the lesson'. This can also be a useful technique when talking to parents, especially those who are used to being dispirited by hearing a long list of misdemeanours, with no positives, about their child.

When we talk about being positive and praising/rewarding, this is really what we mean, rather than the notion that you praise for things which were not actually that good. You find the things, however tiny, that really are good; then it is genuine, gives some hope and something for all concerned to build on.

Keeping a note of ways of differentiating can be really useful and the observations and information gathering that you have done during your visits to your placement school will be invaluable once you start planning for teaching. A number of the standards relate to the ability to make effective use of these insights and information.

> QtT S 3.1.1,
> S3.1.2,
> S3.1.3,
> S3.2.4,
> S3.2.5,
> S3.3.1,
> S3.3.4,
> S3.3.6,
> S3.3.12

Working with other adults in the classroom

The trend towards having more adults in classrooms, rather than just a teacher, has grown rapidly in recent years and the government's workforce remodelling agenda has pushed this forward in a number of ways. For some years there has been a steady increase in the number of adults, both professionals and volunteers, in primary classrooms and working with children and young people with SEN, EAL etc. across the phases.

An early task should be to check the roles of adults who work in the classroom. Some may be present to support a particular pupil (e.g. one who has a statement), but this may well not mean that they stay with that pupil all the time. They may work with the group in which the pupil works or with another group while the teacher spends time with the pupil. Other assistants may have a more general role. Find out what their particular skills and interests are. Having a skilful adult with, for example, an interest in ICT could be an extremely valuable asset.

Where appropriate, and especially where the supporters are experienced and you are comfortable with them, ask for their advice or for feedback. Do phrase this carefully so that you don't end up in a position where you are seen to ignore it, otherwise that positive relationship could be damaged.

Try:

- How do you think X would have responded if I had . . . instead of . . .?
- How do you think Y would respond to/if I . . . working outside the classroom with you . . .?
- I am trying to gather different ideas for recording the red group's ICT progress. Do you have any suggestions?
- How do you usually organise . . .?
- What music generally has a calming effect on the class/pupil X/red group?
- Have the class heard story A/seen this video/ever visited . . .?

QtT S1.6, S3.1.4, S3.3.14

Induction e

It can be potentially difficult to plan for adult support in the classroom especially where the supporter is an experienced professional, but this is an essential part of your teacher training.

The supporter will know the class much better than you, may well be older than you and may be both experienced and well-trained, so establishing a positive working relationship needs sensitive handling on everyone's part. Think about the positive benefits working with this colleague will have and remember that it is a matter of teamwork and recognising and valuing each other's strengths and input.

There are a number of ways you can plan for this support. Most importantly, other adults need to know what your objectives are. What do you want learners to know/to have learnt how to do/to be aware of/to have experienced during this lesson? You should be making this clear to everyone in the classroom, every lesson. Be clear what you would like other adults to do and how much or what type of support you want them to give. Bear in mind that most adults will do what they think best in the absence of any other guidance. If you leave the supporter to do what he/she thinks most appropriate, this may give rise to difficulties for you later. How will you, for example, know what a child or young person has done with and without support and what therefore has been achieved unaided? How will you know what sort of support has been given? It can be very difficult to find time in a busy school day to discuss lesson plans and give feedback but this is of vital importance. Are there other ways you could assist the other adult, e.g. by providing notes or a record sheet of some sort to provide you with feedback?

The opportunity to work in settings other than schools is a very valuable one. QtT S3.1.5 requires that you are able to plan opportunities for pupils to learn in out-of-school contexts and it is possible that you will have the opportunity to accompany a class on a visit outside school while you are on school placement.

Many of the suggestions already made in this chapter will be equally relevant to visits and placements in settings other than schools. There will be some differences, however, and it would be useful to consider what these are and how they impact upon the children/young people and adults and the way in which they work together. Questions you may like to consider are:

- Do the children or young people respond differently to adults who are not school teachers? If so, how? What advantages and disadvantages do adults who are not teachers appear to have?

- How do tasks, activities and environments differ between this setting and school? How did the children/young people respond? What can you learn from this about teaching approaches?

- Are there different opportunities for children with special educational needs, the gifted and talented or EAL children? If you have seen a child in school and now see him/her in another setting, do you see a change in the child's response? If so, how can this observation help you to make his/her learning in school more effective?

- To what extent does the setting take into account the varied needs of children, e.g. those for whom English is an additional language, those with a range of SEN, the gifted and talented etc.? Does the organisation/institution have the equivalent of an SEN policy?

Planning out-of-school visits in a way which ensures all benefit as much as possible is vital. A pre-visit should be undertaken wherever possible and other adults who will be working with the class need to be aware of particular issues, e.g. toileting requirements, space/access required etc. The physical requirements are perhaps the most obvious things to sort out but you will by now be well aware of the other needs that have to be taken into account. Take any opportunity you have of working alongside an experienced teacher who is planning an out-of-school visit. Make notes, ask for copies of checklists and make more notes after the visit so you have a good record. It will be invaluable for future reference.

SEN assignments while on placement

Child studies

You may be required to do some sort of pupil study as part of your training.

Your guidelines may be very specific, e.g. that you must choose a child with EAL, SEN or who is gifted/talented, or it may be a more open brief. It can be tempting to choose a child with a significant and long-term SEN but these children often have many adults supporting them and there is already a lot in their records. It is also easy to get enmeshed in the medical details and to find that this has taken up a lot of your study. Why not choose a pupil whose needs are less severe or obvious? Perhaps one who does not seem to communicate very well, who sits quietly and causes no trouble but is not making much progress, or a learner who really struggles with reading and recording. It is arguably of greater value to you to explore the more common areas of need and difficulty, such as general learning difficulties or behavioural, social and emotional difficulties, than it is to focus on

QtT S1.2,
S1.7, S2.4,
S2.6, S3.1.1,
S3.2.4,
S3.2.5,
S3.2.7

the low-incidence disabilities. As an NQT you will certainly have pupils in your class with these more frequently found needs but it may be years (if ever) before you come across a child with a rare syndrome.

You will have clear guidelines from your ITT provider about your study. These will undoubtedly include issues of confidentiality and who is to see your final study, so be sure you are fully conversant with these. If the guidelines are not clear about confidentiality, ask and check.

The following suggestions may be of help where they do not conflict with the advice and guidance you are given by your ITT provider:

- Background information is needed to give a context but be selective and use only that which is relevant to the study, e.g. what have been identified already as the child's strengths, interests and needs? It is easy to get carried away and use too much of your word count on this part of the study.

- What does the pupil respond well to? How does the pupil respond to specific situations? Examples may be to a new topic, a new physical activity, being faced with a challenge when he/she doesn't know or understand what to do. Does the pupil sit back and not participate, show signs of distress or anxiety or make repeated efforts to succeed?

- Does the pupil's response vary according, for example, to the time of day, how the activity is presented, who presents it, who he/she is sitting or working with? If with a different group, are his/her responses the same?

- What does the pupil enjoy? What are his/her interests? Think about how you can find out about what 'switches' him/her on. Notice the little things like what makes him/her smile or his/her eyes light up.

- How does the pupil appear to learn most effectively? What evidence do you have for this? (Remember to be objective and avoid presenting opinions as facts.)

QtT S3.3.6, S3.3.11 or S3.3.14

Having undertaken your study, find ways of showing that you have taken into account what you have learnt.

Placements in special schools and units

An increasing number of providers are now offering trainees the opportunity to visit special schools and units and, in some cases, to undertake placements. Much of the advice and the suggestions offered earlier in this chapter apply, but there are additional elements to consider as well:

- Many special schools cover a wider age range than mainstream schools.

- While you will meet some children and young people with considerable needs and difficulties, expectations will not be low. Be prepared for considerable levels of achievement in all sorts of fields including the academic, e.g. passing GCSEs.

- This will be an excellent opportunity to see teamwork in action. Staff in special schools have a long tradition and experience of working closely with each other and with other professionals both within and outside of education services.

Responsibilty for pupils with SEN

Three short case studies are provided as a basis for exploring some of the issues raised in this final chapter. You may find it helpful to read them now and then refer back to them as you go through the chapter.

ALEC (YEAR 2)

Alec will soon be moving into Year 3 with a class teacher who will be new to the school. Alec is a lively and highly intelligent little boy with an IQ in the top 2 per cent. He has recently been assessed by the Educational Psychologist, who found him to be particularly able with respect to language and mathematics.

Alec's parents have always been very supportive and determined that he should not become what his mother describes as 'a little professor'. They are immensely proud of him and want the best for him. They have enormous confidence in Alec's current class teacher and teaching assistant, and in the head, but are anxious about how they and Alec will get on with the new teacher and whether she will understand Alec's needs.

KEITH (YEAR 6)

Keith has just moved into Year 6 in his four-class primary school. He has Down's syndrome and a general mental age of 5. Keith is statemented and has, as part of his learning package, 25 hours per week of learning support assistant time.

Keith lives close to the school and seems to be happily settled and reasonably integrated into school and community life. The other children have grown up with him and are used to his rather excitable behaviour. Some of his peers are beginning to find his boisterous interruptions into their playground conversations and football rather irritating but a small group of girls have always 'mothered' him and continue to do so.

Keith's parents are very committed and want him to be happy, well-integrated into the community and to reach his potential. Both parents are absolutely committed to Keith remaining in mainstream school and are now anxious to begin detailed planning and preparations for Keith's move to the local comprehensive school in a year's time. They feel strongly that the LSA who has worked with him since he started school should go with him into his new setting and provide him with some continuity.

The Educational Psychologist has had a discussion with the class teacher and SENCO about Keith's progress and feels that it would be in Keith's interests to have a change of LSA either before or when he moves to the comprehensive school. In the EP's opinion, Keith has become very dependent on his LSA for making his needs known and relies on her to do things he may be able to do independently or at least be encouraged to try himself. Keith's new class teacher can see the EP's point of view but also feels that the LSA would provide some continuity at what will be a time of major change for Keith. The SENCO has been in close contact with her counterpart in the secondary school and is very aware of the considerable concerns that some staff there are expressing about how Keith will cope, the extent to which they will be able to meet his needs and the impact on other pupils' learning.

Keith's annual review takes place shortly and all concerned are anxious that this goes smoothly and that they can agree ways forward.

ELLIE (YEAR 10)

Ellie's parents have been concerned about the increasing amount of time Ellie has spent on homework and, more recently, coursework. Ellie has been frustrated that she doesn't appear able to achieve what she thinks she should be capable of in her written work and has become increasingly anxious and tense. At the suggestion of a family friend she has just been assessed privately by a psychologist and been diagnosed as having 'mild dyslexia'. Ellie's parents immediately wrote to school with the diagnosis and seeking an appointment to discuss it, indicating that they were angry that no-one had ever picked this up before. Ellie was furious that her parents were 'making a fuss' but wanted to know what might help her to get the GCSE results she wants. Several of Ellie's teachers have recently expressed concern that she was at times very quiet and seemed anxious. Her form tutor has broached the subject but Ellie had denied that there were any problems.

A meeting has been set up to be attended by Ellie's parents, the SENCO, Ellie's form tutor and head of year. In the intervening few days between the letter and the meeting, Ellie's parents have become more anxious than angry and are desperate to find a way to support and help Ellie quickly.

Figure 8.3 Case studies – Alec, Keith and Ellie

It is every teacher's responsibility to make effective provision for meeting the needs of pupils with SEN. This will involve making the best possible use of:

- data and information you have access to, e.g. pupil records, IEPs and assessment information, school and local authority policies, school improvement plan, long- and short-term planning, Ofsted reports;

- the support of parents/carers;

- the classroom team, e.g. the teacher(s), teaching assistants, support teachers, technicians etc.;

- out-of-class support, e.g. SENCO, specialist teachers, Educational Psychologist, lunchtime supervisors, speech and language therapist, occupational therapist, education social worker etc.;

- other human resources available to you in the classroom, e.g. parents and other volunteers, trainee teachers, others on work experience or placements, visiting governors etc.;

- the teaching and learning environment(s), e.g. the classroom space itself, other areas that might be used both inside and out, arrangement of resources, additional facilities such as background music and water etc.;

- ICT resources – not only fixed equipment but also portable equipment such as palmtops or laptops, mobile phone technology, digital cameras etc.;

- other resources and materials, e.g. paper-based resources such as books and photocopiable sheets, concrete aids, equipment and tools, displays etc.; and

- your own skills and experience, e.g. in differentiation, communication, demonstration, record keeping etc.

There may be resources that were available to you when you were on school placements that are not available in your first post. Whatever the situation you find yourself in, you will have to work with and maximise what you have available. This does not, of course, mean that you should put up with less than satisfactory or difficult teaching and learning facilities without trying to do something about it; and it does not mean losing sight of the present and what can be achieved while any changes are being made.

Working as part of a team

Induction Standard e

Teamwork has played an enormous part in SEN work for a long time and the importance of this, both within school, education services and between all agencies working with children and young people, has been a strong message from government in recent years. Effective teams do not just happen; team members have to work at this and establish a rapport and respect. You might like to take a few moments to think about what you consider are the key elements of effective teams.

Your list might include:

- recognition of team members' roles and experience;
- recognition of the skills, strengths and interests of team members;
- valuing everyone's contributions; and
- being able to accommodate different views and perspectives.

You might also like to consider what you will bring to a team, both personally and professionally, and how your role in a team might differ now that you have successfully completed training as a teacher, TA or HLTA. Taking opportunities to sit in with and, as appropriate, work with different teams can be extremely valuable. Just watching and listening to an experienced SENCO or EP, for example in an annual review of a statement, can be really worthwhile and can give you some excellent pointers for liaising with parents and developing negotiating skills.

Being able to view an issue from the perspective of other team members is also a necessary skill. As illustrated in some of the case studies in this chapter, professionals do not always agree about priorities or the best way forward but compromises have to be reached and ways forward found and agreed. Being able to understand where others are coming from helps this process.

Working with parents and carers

Induction Standard d

A genuine partnership with parents will make a very positive difference to a child's well-being and progress. (Again, what is good practice in the area of special needs is good practice across the board.) Taking time to establish a positive and trusting relationship with parents will be not only to the child's advantage but also to all those who work with the child in school. If and when any difficulties or problems arise, dealing with them will be considerably easier if there is a rapport between the parents and school staff. If the first time you really meet parents is when things are not going smoothly you can hardly expect your relationship with them to get off to a good start.

It is easier to meet parents of younger children informally, when they collect children from school, for example, than it may be to meet parents of older children or young people. However, many schools do provide facilities for parents to come in to school other than by appointment or at parents' evenings, e.g. social events, drop-in centres, adult learning centres and other community facilities. If your school does not have such facilities, it may be that you could help to set something up.

Communicating with parents does not, of course, always have to take place face-to-face, although there will always be a place for this, especially when establishing a relationship to start with. 'Home books', texting, e-mails, a parents' notice-board, audio tapes, phone messages, digital photos and newsletters can all be helpful tools. Where there are first languages other than English, communication in the appropriate languages is essential. It is important to remember that some parents will have special needs too, and written communications may not necessarily be accessible to all, e.g. there are adults whose literacy skills are weak and who find reading difficult or who don't read nearly as well as those with sensory or physical difficulties. If letters go unanswered it can be easy to forget that there may be a reason other than lack of interest.

It is almost inevitable, though, that there will be some parents who do not, for a variety of reasons, come to the school. In these circumstances, it may be a question of making the best of the situation at the time while looking for alternative ways you might be able to engage with them. It is tempting to think that parents who do not attend parents' evenings are not interested, and sometimes this may appear to be the case. Others, though, may find the thought of coming in to school daunting – a reminder of their own less than positive experience of school – so anything that can be done to make school more welcoming could be of help. In some cases, other education or social service colleagues may know the family and may be able to assist you with information and advice or by acting as an intermediary, if appropriate. The SENCO will be aware of possibilities here. The main thing is to remember that you are not on your own and to seek advice and support.

Many parents of children with SEN are extremely supportive and very committed to ensuring that their child makes the best possible progress. They may have very strong views about what they feel is in their child's best interests and their views may not necessarily accord with yours or the school's, in general; and sometimes parents don't share the same views as each other. Usually, it is possible to find at least a small, non-contentious area that you can all agree on and 'sign up to' to begin with. Frustrating though it may be to start with something that is not your priority and possibly not the parents' either, this may be the best way in which to establish trust and some common ground. An example of this can be found in the case study 'Alex'.

Trying to see things from the parents' perspective is both necessary and helpful. Sometimes you will be working with parents who are finding it difficult to cope or to come to terms with the fact that their child is experiencing difficulties, who are anxious, angry or distressed. At times we need space and time to come to terms with what is being suggested or the situation with which we are faced, while at others we just want to get on with moving forward. Some people instinctively sense the appropriate response while others have to work at this rather more. You need to develop that sensitivity as well as tact and diplomacy, which come more naturally to some than to others.

Do not be afraid to call on the advice and support of colleagues rather than trying to cope on your own. There are times when this is absolutely essential and, if ever in doubt, do whatever you can to ensure that you do not meet parents on your own.

SEN report writing

You will be asked to provide reports, whether formal or informal, at various times when you have children with SEN in your class(es). Your skills of observation and assessment, as well as up-to-date and effective record keeping, will assist enormously. The following tips may be useful pointers as well:

- Be clear as to the purpose of the report and who the audience is.
- Keep it simple and avoid educational jargon.
- Be objective (this is not the place for speculation or interpretation of, for example, what a child might have been thinking at the time of an incident).
- Provide examples to support a point.
- Avoid the anecdotal.
- Avoid long lists of daily occurrences and misdemeanours (unless specifically asked to record these, in which case brevity and clarity are key).
- Keep it as short as possible while still making the message clear. Readers will not want to spend time reading an essay.

Report writing is a skill like any other and practice will make perfect.

Working with children and young people with special educational needs can be one of the most rewarding aspects of teaching and supporting. If this book has taken you any further along the road of making a real difference to this group of learners as part of the wider learning community it will have succeeded in its aims. This is just the start of one of the most exciting journeys you can make.

REFLECTION POINTS

Thinking about some of the following questions before going on a school placement can help you to be well-prepared, focused and confident:

1. As a trainee teacher, how would you respond if it was suggested that having you in the classroom would be detrimental to the progress of children with special educational needs? What arguments could you present that would show that a trainee teacher in the classroom was beneficial to all pupils including those with SEN?

2. What steps could (a) a class/subject teacher and (b) a SENCO take to ensure that the training you received while on placement prepared you as effectively as possible for teaching in an inclusive classroom?

3. If you were told that half your placement class have SEN and English is not the first language for the majority, how would you respond? Would you see this as a positive challenge and an exciting opportunity even if tinged with some apprehensions and anxieties about your capabilities? Would you see it as a chance to demonstrate that you were working towards or reaching QTS standards, or would you see it as being harder or perhaps unfair because you were less likely than some of your peers in other schools to get a good assessment grade, due to the fact that the children would be more difficult to teach? What would help you to approach this placement with more confidence and less anxiety?

4. Your subject specialism(s). Think about the particular difficulties children or young people may experience with your subject and what particular solutions may be. Keep a file of ideas for differentiated activities, teaching approaches, vocabulary etc.

Appendix A: Standards information

Qualifying to Teach – the professional standards for the award of QTS in England

In January 2002, *Qualifying to Teach* (QtT), the document detailing the new standards for the award of Qualified Teacher Status (QTS) and the requirements of Initial Teacher Training (ITT), was published (DfES/Teacher Training Agency (2001)). These standards and requirements came into force in September 2002 and all trainee teachers in England now work towards these in order to be awarded QTS.

In the introduction to *Qualifying to Teach* it is made clear that the standards are outcome statements which describe the criteria for the award of Qualified Teacher Status (QTS). In other words, the standards indicate what you should be able to do and to demonstrate if you are to be awarded QTS. The three interrelated sections – Professional Values and Practice; Knowledge and Understanding; and Teaching apply to all trainees. A number of the standards make specific or implicit reference to special educational needs (1.1, 2.4, 2.6, 3.1.1, 3.1.2, 3.1.4, 3.2.4, 3.3.1, 3.3.4, 3.3.13, 3.3.14), children for whom English is an additional language (1.1, 1.6, 2.4, 3.1.2, 3.2.5, 3.3.1, 3.3.5, 3.3.6, 3.3.13) or who are gifted and talented (3.3.4). However, it would be a mistake to see these as the only relevant standards in the context of this book or of special educational needs. *Qualifying to Teach* is about meeting the needs of *all* children regardless of their learning styles, needs, culture and background and this underpins all the standards.

Professional Standards for Higher Level Teaching Assistants (HLTAs) – England

As with the QTS standards, the HLTA standards are grouped in three interrelated sections – Professional Values and Practice; Knowledge and Understanding; and Teaching and Learning Activities. It is made clear in the standards that the roles of teachers and HLTAs are not interchangeable. However, the standards have been designed 'to support smooth progression to QTS' for those HLTAs who may want to go on to train as teachers.

For further information about Initial Teacher Training, NQT induction or teaching in different parts of the UK please refer to the relevant bodies below.

England

Training and Development Agency for schools (previously the Teacher Training Agency): TDA, Portland House, Bressenden Place, London SW1E 5TT

Information about Initial Teacher Training and the induction of newly qualified teachers (NQTs) in England can be found on the website (www.tda.gov.uk). The website is the primary source of information and has downloadable materials and resources including the induction standards, career entry and development profile (CEDP) documentation, support materials and video clips.

Northern Ireland

Department of Education (Teachers Branch), Waterside House, 75 Duke Street, Londonderry BT47 6FP
www.deni.gov.uk/index.htm

Scotland

General Teaching Council for Scotland, Clerwood House, 96 Clermiston Road, Edinburgh EH12 6UT
Tel: 0131 314 6000
E-mail: induction@gtcs.org.uk

The GTC for Scotland administers the probation period (induction) for NQTs. The website (www.gtcs.org.uk) gives information about the probation period, the Teacher Induction Scheme and alternative routes to registration.

Wales

Training and Education Department, Welsh National Assembly, Cardiff Bay, Cardiff CF99 1NA
www.wales.gov.uk

Appendix B: Individual Education Plans

Examples of IEPs

The examples in this appendix are taken from IEPs and are intended as samples of targets and target-setting formats for discussion and reflection rather than complete IEPs or examples of best practice.

Table B1   Example of a target and a target-setting format for a Primary IEP at SA

Individual Education Plan for:		Stage: SA	
Year/Class:		DOB:	
Area(s) of concern: Literacy			
Focus for this plan: Understanding of everyday concepts			
Date of IEP:		Review date:	

Target (must be SMART, i.e. specific, measurable, achievable, realistic and timed)	Achievement criteria	Resources and strategies	Results
Jason will be able to identify objects that are 'big' or 'small' and that are 'hard' or 'soft'	Jason will be able to point out or give objects that are big or small or hard or soft on at least three separate and random occasions during the final week of the four-week programme	TA and class teacher plus any other adults in the classroom will make a point of using the terms in context and of reinforcing the terms. Provision of play opportunities with objects that can be described using these terms. Parents will do the same at home. TA will work with Jason for five minutes every day on these concepts. Weekly meeting on Thursdays with teacher, TA and mother to review progress.	Target for big and small was achieved in week 3. Target for hard and soft achieved in week 4.

Table B2 Example of targets and a target-setting format for a secondary IEP at SA+

Targets	Success criteria	Strategies and resources	Provision (who will do what and when)	Evaluation
Sonia will use correct punctuation and paragraphs in her writing.	Five pieces of work with correct punctuation and use of paragraphs during this four-week period	• Writing frames and story boards. • Talk about content before starting writing (e.g. to TA). • Prompt sheet with punctuation reminders and pictorial representation of paragraphs. • Appropriate computer programs as suggested by EP and SENCO.	MF will consult subject staff to identify written work that could contribute to this target. TA to prompt as appropriate. Record sheet in learning resource office to be updated weekly by TA.	Target exceeded: 8 pieces of work with the correct punctuation and use of paragraphs were completed: 4 for English, 2 for History, 1 for Geography and 1 for Citizenship.
Sonia will discuss the main characters in *Of Mice and Men.*	On at least three occasions during a four-week period	• Opportunities provided during small-group time and during homework club.	TA and teacher as appropriate. CD to provide opportunities in homework club.	

Signed:

Pupil: Form tutor:

SENCO: Parent/carer:

Table B3 Example of Early Years IEP target-setting format

Nature of difficulty	SMART target	Success criteria	Strategies and resources required	Review
David doesn't play with other children or like them near him while he is playing on his own.	David will play with Mandy (nursery nurse) with another child playing close by.	The target behaviour is observed for a period of five minutes or more for three consecutive sessions.	Mandy will play with David for ten–fifteen minutes during each session and encourage him and another child to play closer to each other. Mandy will liaise with David's mother after each session.	Review date set for three weeks' time to be attended by nursery teacher, nursery nurse (Mandy) and David's mother.

Appendix C: Acronyms

Glossary of acronyms

ADHD – Attention Deficit (Hyperactivity) Disorder
ASD – Autistic Spectrum Disorder
EAL – English as an Additional Language
EP – Educational Psychologist
EYA – Early Years Action
EYA+ – Early Years Action Plus
GEP – Group Education Plan
GLD – general/global learning difficulties
GTP – Graduate Teacher Programme
HLTA – Higher Level Teaching Assistant
ICT – Information and communication technology
IEP – Individual Education Plan
IS – Induction Standards – the professional standards for NQTs in England
ITT – Initial Teacher Training
LEA – local education authority
LM – learning mentor
LSA – learning support assistant
NQT – newly qualified teacher
QTS – Qualified Teacher Status
QtT – Qualifying to Teach – the professional standards for qualified teacher status in England
SA – School Action
SA+ – School Action Plus
SCITT – School-centred initial teacher training
SEN – special educational needs
SENCO – special educational needs co-ordinator
TA – teaching assistant

Resources and further reading

Resources and suggestions for further reading have been grouped by topic.

Able children (see Gifted and talented)

Accelerated learning

Network Educational Press (www.networkpress.co.uk).

Further reading

Buzan, T. (2002) *How to Mind Map*. London: Thorsons.

Caviglioli, O. and Harris, I. (2000) *Mapwise*. Stafford: Network Educational Press.

Smith, A. (1996) *Accelerated Learning in the Classroom*. Stafford: Network Educational Press.

Smith, A. (1998) *Accelerated Learning in Practice* (2nd edn). Stafford: Network Educational Press.

Smith, A., Lovatt, M. and Wise, D. (2003) *Accelerated Learning: A User's Guide*. Stafford: Network Educational Press.

Asthma

Further reading

Hull Learning Services (2004) *Supporting Children with Asthma*. London: David Fulton Publishers.

Attention Deficit (Hyperactivity) Disorder (ADD and ADHD)

Further reading

Cooper, P. and Ideus, K. (1996) *Attention Deficit Hyperactivity Disorder: A Practical Guide for Teachers*. London: David Fulton Publishers.

Cooper, P. and O'Regan, F. J. (2001) *Educating Children with AD/HD: A Teacher's Manual*. London: RoutledgeFalmer.

Kewley, G. (2005) *Attention Deficit Hyperactivity Disorder: What Can Teachers Do?* (2nd edn). London: David Fulton Publishers.

Autistic spectrum disorders

DfES SEN website (www.dfes.gov.uk/sen).

National Autistic Society (www.nas.org.uk).

Further reading

DfES (2002) *The Good Practice Guidance on Autistic Spectrum Disorders.* London: DfES.

Hull Learning Services (2004) *Supporting Children with Autistic Spectrum Disorder.* London: David Fulton Publishers.

Jordan, R. and Powell, S. (1995) *Understanding and Teaching Children with Autism.* New York: Wiley.

Wing, L. (1995) *Autistic Spectrum Disorders: An Aid to Diagnosis* (3rd edn). London: National Autistic Society.

Behavioural, emotional and social difficulties (see also Classroom management)

Association of Workers for Children with EBD (www.sebda.org).

Behaviour4Learning (www.behaviour4learning.ac.uk).

HTI (Heads, Teachers and Industry) (www.what-next.org.uk).

Further reading

Long, R. and Fogell, J. (1999) *Supporting Pupils with Emotional Difficulties.* London: David Fulton Publishers.

Mitchell, G. (2001) *Practical Strategies for Individual Behaviour Difficulties.* London: David Fulton Publishers.

Cerebral palsy

SCOPE (www.scope.org.uk).

Further reading

Hull Learning Services (2004) *Supporting Children with Cerebral Palsy.* London: David Fulton Publishers.

Classroom management

Further reading

McNamara, E. (1999) *Positive Pupil Management and Motivation.* London: David Fulton Publishers.

Rogers, W. (2000) *Classroom Behaviour: A Practical Guide to Effective Teaching, Behaviour Management and Colleague Support.* London: Books Education.

Roffey, S. and O'Reirdan, T. (1997) *Infant Classroom Behaviour.* London: David Fulton Publishers.

Visser, J. (2000) *Managing Behaviour in Classrooms.* London: David Fulton Publishers.

Classroom support

Further reading

Cowne, E. with Murphy, M. (2001) *Beginner's Guide to Meeting Special Educational Needs: A Handbook.* Tamworth: NASEN.

Fox, G. (1998) *A Handbook for Learning Support Assistants.* London: David Fulton Publishers.

Lorenz, S. (1998) *Effective In-Class Support*. London: David Fulton Publishers.

MacKinnon, C. (2002) *Teaching Strategies and Resources: A Practical Guide for Primary Teachers and Classroom Assistants*. London: David Fulton Publishers.

Cystic fibrosis

Cystic Fibrosis Trust (www.cftrust.org.uk).

Diabetes

British Diabetic Association UK (www.diabetes.org.uk).

Disability (general)

Disability Alliance (www.disabilityalliance.org.uk).

Disability Equality in Education (www.diseed.org.uk).

Disability Sport England (www.disabilitysport.org.uk).

Further reading
Barton, L. (2001) *Disability, Politics and the Struggle for Change*. London: David Fulton Publishers.

Down's syndrome

The Down's Syndrome Association (www.dsa-uk.com).

Further reading
Hull Learning Services (2004) *Supporting Children with Down's Syndrome*. London: David Fulton Publishers.

Dyslexia

British Dyslexia Association (BDA) (www.bdadyslexia.org.uk).

Dyslexia Institute (www.dyslexia-inst.org.uk).

Mind Games programme and applications (www.mindgamessolutions.com).

Further reading
Hannell, G. (2004) *Dyslexia: Action Plans for Successful Learning*. London: David Fulton Publishers.

Hull Learning Services (2004) *Supporting Children with Dyslexia*. London: David Fulton Publishers.

Ott, P. (1997) *How to Detect and Manage Dyslexia*. Oxford: Heinemann Educational Publishers.

Reid, G. (2005) *Dyslexia and Inclusion*. London: David Fulton Publishers.

Dyspraxia

Dyspraxia Foundation (www.dyspraxiafoundation.org.uk).

LDA (www.ldalearning.com).

Further reading

Hull Learning Services (2004) *Supporting Children with Motor Co-ordination Difficulties*. London: David Fulton Publishers.

Portwood, M. (2000) *Understanding Developmental Dyspraxia*. London: David Fulton Publishers.

Early Years and SEN

Drifte, C. (2002) *Early Learning Goals for Children with Special Needs*. London: David Fulton Publishers.

Glenn, A., Cousins, J. and Helps, A. (2005) *Removing Barriers to Learning in the Early Years*. London: David Fulton Publishers.

Jones, P. (2005) *Inclusion in the Early Years: Stories of Good Practice*. London: David Fulton Publishers.

Roffey, S. (2001) *Special Needs in the Early Years* (2nd edn). London: David Fulton Publishers.

Spencer, C. and Schnelling, K. (2002) *Handbook for Pre-School SEN Provision* (2nd edn). London: David Fulton Publishers.

SureStart (2003) *SEN Training Materials: SureStart SEN Training Pack*. Nottingham: DfES.

English as an Additional Language (EAL)

DfES (www.standards.dfes.gov.uk/ethnicminorities/).

Multiverse (www.multiverse.ac.uk).

Further reading

Gardner, P. (2001) *Teaching and Learning in Multicultural Classrooms*. London: David Fulton Publishers.

Gardner, P. (2002) *Strategies and Resources for Teaching and Learning in Inclusive Classrooms*. London: David Fulton Publishers.

Haslam, E., Kellet, E. and Wilkin, Y. (2004) *English as an Additional Language*. London: David Fulton Publishers.

Ofsted (1999) *Raising the Attainment of Ethnic Minority Pupils*. London: Ofsted.

QCA (2000) *A Language in Common: Assessing English as an Additional Language*. London: QCA.

Epilepsy

British Epilepsy Association (www.epilepsy.org.uk).

National Society for Epilepsy (www.epilepsynse.org.uk).

Further reading

Hull Learning Services (2004) *Supporting Children with Epilepsy*. London: David Fulton Publishers.

Exclusion

Teachernet (www.teachernet.gov.uk/exclusion).

Further reading

DfES (2003) *The Education (Pupils' Exclusions and Appeals) (Maintained Schools) (England) Regulations 2002 (S.1.2002/3178)*. Nottingham: DfES.

DfES (2003) *The Education (Pupils' Exclusions and Appeals) (Pupil Referral Units) (England) Regulations 2002 (S.1.2002/3179)*. Nottingham: DfES.

DfES (2004) *Improving Behaviour and Attendance: Guidance on Exclusion from Schools and Pupil Referral Units (DfES/0354/2004)*. Nottingham: DfES.

Gifted and talented

DfES (www.standards.dfes.gov.uk/giftedandtalented).

National Association for Able Children in Education (NACE) (www.nace.co.uk).

National Association for Gifted Children (NAGC) (www.nagc.org).

Qualifications and Curriculum Authority (QCA) (www.qca.org.uk).

World Class Arena (www.worldclassarena.org.uk).

Further reading

DfEE (2000) *National Literacy and Numeracy Strategies: Guidance on Teaching Able Children*. London: DfEE.

Eyre, D. (1997) *Able Children in Ordinary Schools*. London: David Fulton Publishers.

Koshy, V. (2002) *Teaching Gifted Children 4–7*. London: David Fulton Publishers.

Lee-Corbin, H. and Denicolo, P. (1998) *Recognising and Supporting Able Children in Primary Schools*. London: David Fulton Publishers.

QCA (2001) *Working with Gifted and Talented Children*. London: QCA.

Teare, B. (1997) *Effective Provision for Able and Talented Children* (2nd edn). Stafford: Network Educational Press.

Wallace, B. (2000) *Teaching the Very Able Child*. London: David Fulton Publishers in association with NACE.

Government circulars, guidance and legislation (in chronological order)

DFE (1994) *Code of Practice on the Identification and Assessment of Special Educational Needs*. London: DFE.

DfEE (1997) *Excellence for All Children: Meeting Special Educational Needs*. Sudbury: DfEE.

DfEE (1998) *Meeting Special Educational Needs: A Programme for Action*. Sudbury: DfEE.

DfEE (1999) Circular 10/99: *Social Inclusion: Pupil Support*. Sudbury: DfEE.

DfEE (1999) *The National Curriculum Handbook: Inclusion: Providing Effective Learning Opportunities for All Pupils*. Sudbury: DfEE.

DfES (2001) *Inclusive Schooling: Children with Special Educational Needs*. London: DfES.

DfES (2001) *SEN Code of Practice*. London: DfES.

DfES (2003) *Every Child Matters*. London: DfES.

DfES (2004) *Removing Barriers to Achievement*. London: DfES.

DfES (2004) *Five Year Strategy for Children and Learners*. London: DfES.

DfES/Teacher Training Agency (2001) *Qualifying to Teach*. London: TTA.

DfES/Teacher Training Agency (2002) *Qualifying to Teach Handbook of Guidance Autumn 2002*. London: TTA.

Hearing impairment (see Sensory)

Higher Level Teaching Assistants

HLTA website (www.hlta.gov.uk).

Further reading

DfES/TTA (2004) *Professional Standards for Higher Level Teaching Assistants*. London: TTA.

Watkinson, A. (2005) *Professional Values and Practice: The Essential Guide for Higher Level Teaching Assistants*. London: David Fulton Publishers.

ICT

British Educational Communication Technology Agency (BECTA) (www.becta.org.uk).

Crick Software Ltd (www.cricksoft.com).

iAnsyst Ltd (www.iansyst.co.uk).

Inclusive Technology Ltd (www.inclusive.co.uk).

Numbershark (www.numbershark.co.uk).

R-E-M (www.r-e-m.co.uk).

Wordshark (www.wordshark.co.uk).

Further reading

Banes, D. and Walter, R. (2002) *Internet for All*. London: David Fulton Publishers.

Flavell, E., Singleton, L. and Ross, I. (2004) *Access to ICT: Curriculum Planning and Practical Activities for Pupils with Learning Difficulties*. London: David Fulton Publishers.

Gage, J. (2005) *How to Use an Interactive Whiteboard Really Effectively in Your Primary Classroom*. London: David Fulton Publishers.

Taylor, N. and Chacksfield, J. (2005) *ICT for Learners with Special Needs*. London: David Fulton Publishers.

Inclusion

Alliance for Inclusive Education (www.allfie.org.uk).

Disability Equality in Education (www.diseed.org.uk).

National Grid for Learning (NGfL) (www.inclusion.ngfl.gov.uk).

Parents for Inclusion (www.parentsforinclusion.org).

Further reading

Ainscow, M. (1999) *Understanding the Development of Inclusive Schools*. London: Falmer Press.

Billington, T. (2000) *Separating, Losing and Excluding Children: Narratives of Difference*. London: RoutledgeFalmer.

Booth, T. and Ainscow, M. (2000) *Index for Inclusion: Developing Learning and Participation in Schools*. Bristol: CSIE.

Carpenter, B., Ashdown, R. and Bovair, K. (2001) *Enabling Access* (2nd edn). London: David Fulton Publishers.

Cheminais, R. (2004) *How to Create an Inclusive Classroom*. London: David Fulton Publishers.

DfEE (1999) Circular 10/99: *Social Inclusion: Pupil Support*. London: DfEE.

DfEE (1999) *The National Curriculum Handbook: Inclusion: Providing Effective Learning Opportunities for All Pupils*. London: DfEE.

DfES (2001) *Inclusive Schooling: Children with Special Educational Needs*. London: DfES.

Farrell, M. (2000) 'Educational inclusion and raising standards'. *British Journal of Special Education*, 27(1), March.

NASEN *Inclusion Policy* (www.nasen.org.uk).

National Curriculum (2000) *Inclusion Statement* (www.nc.gov.uk.net).

Ofsted (2000) *Evaluating Educational Inclusion: Guidance for Inspectors and Schools*. London: Ofsted.

Thomas, G. and Loxley, A. (2001) *Deconstructing Special Education and Constructing Inclusion*. Buckingham: Open University Press.

UNESCO (1994) *The Salamanca Statement for Action on Special Educational Needs*. Paris: UNESCO.

Warnock (2005) *Special Educational Needs: A New Look (No. 11 in a series of policy discussions)*. Canterbury: Philosophy of Education Society of Great Britain.

Wearmouth, J. (ed.) (2001) *Special Educational Provision in the Context of Inclusion* London: David Fulton Publishers/Open University.

Learning difficulties (general)

Mencap (www.mencap.org.uk).

The National Association for Mental Health (MIND) (www.mind.org.uk).

Further reading

Beveridge, S. (1996) *Spotlight on Special Educational Needs: Learning Difficulties*. Stafford: NASEN.

Westwood, P. (2004) *Learning and Learning Difficulties: A Handbook for Teachers*. London: David Fulton Publishers.

Westwood, P. (2004) *Numeracy and Learning Difficulties: Approaches to Teaching and Assessment*. London: David Fulton Publishers.

Medical conditions

Further reading

Closs, A. (ed.) (1999) *The Education of Children with Medical Conditions*. London: David Fulton Publishers.

DfEE (1996) *Supporting Pupils with Medical Needs*. London: DfEE.

Hull Learning Services (2004) *Supporting Children with Medical Conditions*. London: David Fulton Publishers.

Muscular dystrophy

Muscular Dystrophy Campaign (www.muscular-dystrophy.org.uk).

Self-esteem

Lucky Duck Publishing Ltd (www.luckyduck.co.uk).

Further reading
Smith, A. (1996) *Accelerated Learning in the Classroom*. Stafford: Network Educational Press.

Sensory

The National Deaf Children's Society (www.ndcs.org.uk).

Royal National Institute for the Blind (RNIB) (www.rnib.org.uk/).

Royal National Institute for the Deaf (RNID) (www.rnid.org.uk).

Further reading
Mason, H. (1995) *Spotlight on Special Educational Needs: Visual Impairment*. Tamworth: NASEN.

Watson, L. (1996) *Spotlight on Special Educational Needs: Hearing Impairment*. Tamworth: NASEN.

Special educational needs (general)

British Institute of Learning Disabilities (BILD) (www.bild.org.uk).

David Fulton Publishers (www.fultonpublishers.co.uk).

Department for Education and Skills (DfES) SEN website (www.dfes.gov.uk/sen).

National Association of Special Educational Needs (NASEN) (www.nasen.org.uk).

Special Educational Needs and Disability Tribunal

Special Educational Needs Tribunal (www.sendist.gov.uk).

Specific learning difficulties (see also Dyslexia)

British Dyslexia Association (BDA) (www.bda-dyslexia.org.uk).

iANSYST (Cambridge) (www.dyslexic.com).

LDA (www.ldalearning.com).

Further reading
Smith, D. (1996) *Spotlight on Special Educational Needs: Specific Learning Difficulties*. Tamworth: NASEN.